Longman
PHOTO
DICTIONARY

Teacher's
Guide

John N. Rosenthal
Marilyn S. Rosenthal

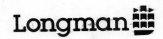

Longman Photo Dictionary Teacher's Guide

Copyright © 1989, by Longman Inc.

Longman, Inc.
95 Church Street
White Plains, N.Y. 10601

Associated companies: Longman Group Ltd., London; Longman Cheshire Pty., Melbourne; Longman Paul Pty., Auckland; Copp Clark Pitman, Toronto; Pitman Publishing Inc., New York

ISBN   0-8013-0318-4

89 90 91 92 9 8 7 6 5 4 3 2 1

Distributed in the United Kingdom by Longman Group Ltd., Longman House, Burnt Hill, Harlow, Essex CM20 2JE, England, and by associated companies, branches and representatives throughout the world.

CONTENTS

INTRODUCTION

The Longman Photo Dictionary Vocabulary and Conversation Program is a complete, comprehensive program that teaches basic vocabulary and conversation to adults and young adults. It also provides a basic resource of North American language and culture, which can be used on various levels as either a main or supplementary teaching tool.

COMPONENTS OF THE PROGRAM

The Longman Photo Dictionary

This is the core of the program. The dictionary presents more than 2000 high-frequency vocabulary words in more than 80 semantic contexts. The four color photographs throughout the book provide a realistic panorama of language and life in North America.

It is not a dictionary in the traditional sense, where students look up the meaning of words. It is, rather, a vocabulary and conversation practice book in which essential vocabulary for teaching everyday conversation is presented contextually through realistic photographs.

A Mini-Practice in each unit is designed to stimulate conversation and guide the students in describing the scenes or in using the vocabulary to communicate about their own lives and opinions. The particular structure selected for each Mini-Practice is intrinsically related to its generalized use in the context of the photographs and vocabulary in each unit. For example, the unit, Fast Food and Snacks, uses the structure "Do you like hot dogs?" as the obvious structure for having students express their preferences about the items in the unit.

The units of the dictionary are self-contained and are not presented in a developmental order. We encourage you to introduce the units in a way that suits your particular teaching situation best.

Workbooks and Cassettes

The Longman Photo Dictionary Workbooks come in three levels of difficulty, each with its own accompanying listening-practice cassette. The purpose of the workbooks is to reinforce and expand the student's ability to use and understand the vocabulary and structures presented in the Longman Photo Dictionary. All workbooks can be used in class, for homework, or self-study. There are between one and three workbook pages for every unit of the *Longman Photo Dictionary*.

The *Pronunciation and Spelling Workbook* is intended to help pre-beginners (or simply those who need it) to associate the spoken and written forms of the words in the *Longman Photo Dictionary*. The accompanying cassette gives students practice in listening, repeating, and spelling the words. Dictations, fill-ins, and matching exercises reinforce sound/symbol correspondence.

The *Beginning Workbook* and the *Intermediate Workbook* contain task listening exercises for each unit. These real-life listening tasks are on accompanying cassettes and give the student the opportunity to understand the *Longman Photo Dictionary* vocabulary in the context of everyday conversational English. Practical writing tasks and a wealth of varied activities including matching, completion, and fill-in exercises, as well as games and puzzles, build confidence and reinforce learning.

Wall Charts

There are two sets of 25 full-color wall charts, which are reproduced and enlarged pages from the Longman Photo Dictionary. These 16 x 20 charts are sturdy and durable so that they can have repeated use in the classroom. They are intended for practice with pairs of students and small groups. On the back of each wall chart is a list of all the words and the Mini-Practice from the corresponding *Longman Photo Dictionary* page. In addition, there is an individual teacher's guide called Further Practice on the back of each chart giving extensive suggestions to practice the words. Further Practice includes additional structures to use with the vocabulary, topics for discussions, role plays, games, and activities. These suggested activities are graded by level (* = easy, ** = more difficult) so that the charts may be used with different levels of students.

SET I

NUMBERS	TIME	WEATHER & SEASONS
FRUIT	VEGETABLES	FAST FOOD & SNACKS
OCCUPATIONS	THE BODY	ACTION AT HOME
ACTION AT THE GYM	ACTION AT SCHOOL	EMOTIONS
OPPOSITES	THE LIVING ROOM	THE KITCHEN
KITCHENWARE	THE TRAIN, BUS & TAXI	ROUTES & ROAD SIGNS
SPECTATOR SPORTS	THE ZOO AND PETS	

SET II

CALENDAR & HOLIDAYS	SHAPES & MEASUREMENTS	THE UNITED STATES
CANADA	THE SUPERMARKET	THE OFFICE
THE DOCTOR	THE DENTIST	MEN'S WEAR
WOMEN'S WEAR	HOUSING	THE DINING ROOM
THE LAUNDRY ROOM	TOOLS	ELECTRONICS
LAND & WATER	THE BEACH	WATER SPORTS
WINTER SPORTS	OTHER SPORTS	THE FARM
FISH & SEA ANIMALS		

The Further Practice sections are also reproduced in this *Teacher's Guide*, along with Further Practice for the remaining pages of the *Longman Photo Dictionary*.

TEACHER'S GUIDE

General Suggestions

The primary objective in using the *Longman Photo Dictionary* is to teach the students to recognize and pronounce the vocabulary items on the page and to associate them with meaning (expressed in the photographs). There are many ways to present the vocabulary, depending on the age, cultural background, and language level of your students. We suggest the following steps. You may choose others or only some of these:

1. Recognition: Pronounce each word (in a normal conversational manner) while pointing to the appropriate photo. Students may point along in their own books or may point to the photos on the chart as you say each word. You can make a memory game of recognition out of this, speeding up and slowing down to vary the pace. You may want to present a few items at a time or do the entire page, depending on the attention span of your students.

2. Repetition: Once the students have heard and recognized the words, they are now ready to practice repeating them. Say each word and have the students repeat chorally first. (This helps the shy ones.) Then, call on students individually to repeat each word. Continue pointing to the appropriate photo as you say each word and they repeat it. A variation of this, after they have repeated after you, is for students to do this same thing in pairs or groups. One student says the word and points to the photo, and the group or the other student repeats the word. Vary the pace.

3. *Association*: Once the students are able to pronounce the words, check their pronunciation to be sure that they are associating the words with the appropriate photo and, in some cases, that they associate the photos with the written words. There are many ways to do this. You can point to the item (photo) on the chart or in the book and have students call out the word chorally or individually. Students can also do this with each other. You can then reverse the process and (with students in pairs or small groups) have one student say the item and the other student point to the appropriate photo. Another variation in the association process is to have students write the appropriate word as you or another student point to the photo. One student could be doing this at the board. Still another variation is a simple dictation, with you or a student pronouncing the word while the other students write what you have said.

4. *Mini-Practice*: The Mini-Practice in each unit provides the structure for the students to describe or discuss the items on the page. You may first want to do the Mini-Practice aloud with one student and then have students practice together in pairs or groups. Some of the conventions used in the Mini Practice are as follows: a slash mark as in "Yes, I do./No, I don't." indicates that students have an alternative and should give their opinions. The dots . . . indicate that students should create their own statements or questions and answers based on the model given.

Unit by Unit Suggestions and Information

Primary Objectives: This section lists the objectives with respect to the specific vocabulary and Mini-Practice.

Conversational Objectives: This section lists the conversational objectives, relating the topics to the students' lives. Activities that fulfill these objectives are listed in the Further Practice sections.

Related Units: This section lists other units in the Longman Photo Dictionary that are related semantically to the unit being presented. For example, you may want to refer to part of the related unit, Kitchenware, when presenting the unit, The Kitchen.

Cultural Comments: It has often been said that teaching the language is teaching the culture. This section presents notes about North American culture as it relates to the unit. These comments are based on a socio-linguistic perspective and try to explain the cultural context of the language. For example, in The Kitchen, the notes mention that the kitchen is often a gathering place for discussions with family and close friends. Sometimes these notes refer to specific cultural values that provide important background information, and often they refer to mainstream survival information. For example, the Time unit mentions that promptness is very important in our culture, particularly in business appointments and job interviews.

Vocabulary Notes: This section presents three types of linguistic information: Alternate Words, Usage, and Additional Words.

Alternate Words are other words that can be substituted for those in the unit. Often, these are particular geographical or social variants.

Usage includes pronunciation and grammar notes, and comments on how certain words are used. Sometimes, related slang is listed and labeled here.

Additional Words are other words that are not on the page but might occur in conversation about the unit topic. For example, "silverware" is listed as an additional word in DINING ROOM.

Related Idioms and Expressions: Two types of idioms are presented in this Teacher's Guide: contextual idioms and referential idioms.

Contextual idioms are those whose meaning relates to the semantic context of the words on the page. The individual words of the idiom are often completely unlike the words on the page in form. For example, "house call" (meaning when a doctor comes to your house because you are too sick to go to the doctor's office) is presented in the unit, The Doctor, as a contextual idiom.

Referential idioms are those whose individual words are similar in form to the vocabulary in the unit, even though the meaning has nothing in common with the specific vocabulary of the unit. For example, "to put your foot in your mouth" (meaning to say something innocently that ends up being harmful to yourself) is presented in The Body unit as a referential idiom.

Mini-Practice Notes: This section presents three types of information about the Mini-Practices: Additional Structures, Usage notes, and Alternate Structures.

Further Practice: This section presents numerous ideas for additional practice with other structures as well as extensive suggestions for discussions, role plays, games, and activities. The Further Practice Sections for each unit of the Longman Photo Dictionary are in this Teacher's Guide. They are also reproduced on the reverse side of the Wall charts, Sets I and II.

We have tried to be as exhaustive as possible in describing ways to use the Longman Photo Dictionary from presentation to reinforcement to expansion. We have also tried to guide you in making useful statements to your students about the language and culture. We know that you will find still other creative ways to use the Longman Photo Dictionary Vocabulary and Conversation Program in your classes, depending on your particular situation. The possibilities are limitless.

PRIMARY OBJECTIVES

Count in sequence from 1 to 100.
Recognize and use numbers from 1 to 100, thousands, ten thousands, and millions.
Perform simple mathematical operations of addition, subtraction, multiplication, and
　　division with numbers, fractions, and percentages.

CONVERSATIONAL OBJECTIVES

Use numbers in conversations about age and money.
Recognize and use percentages and fractions.
Play Bingo, cards.

RELATED UNITS

Time (page 2), Calendar & Holidays (page 3), Shapes & Measurements (page 5), Money &
　　Banking (page 6)

CULTURAL COMMENTS

Direct questions about age, salary, and how much someone's house or car cost are personal
　　and private information. It is considered rude for casual acquaintances to ask such
　　information.

VOCABULARY NOTES

Additional Words

Introduce ordinals *fifth* through *thirtieth* (see Further Practice for **Calendar & Holidays**, page 7).
You may want to teach these additional ordinals: fortieth (40th), fiftieth (50th), sixtieth
　　(60th), seventieth (70th), eightieth (80th), ninetieth (90th), one hundredth (100th). Note
　　that ordinals between *thirtieth* and *one hundredth* use the pattern used in *twentieth*
　　through *twenty-ninth*.

Usage

Have students distinguish among the following numbers which sound similar:
13/30; 14/40; 15/50; 16/60; 17/70; 18/80; 19/90; 13/15/16; 13th/30th/38th; 14th/40th/48th;
　　15th/50th/58th/; 16th/60th/68th; 17th/70th/78th; 18th/80th/88th; 19th/90th/98th; 20th/
　　28th; 13th/15th/16th.

RELATED IDIOMS AND EXPRESSIONS

to count on: to expect something (good or bad) from someone or something.
six of one, half dozen of the other: when two alternatives have the same or a similar result.
Two's company, three's a crowd: a situation where two people prefer to be alone together,
　　not with a third person.

1

MINI-PRACTICE NOTES

Usage

The mini-practice introduces the structure "How much is . . . ?" with mathematical operations. Expand the use of the structure to "How much is it?" (for use with singular nouns) and "How much are they?" (with plural nouns).

> I like that <u>shirt</u>. How much is it?
> It's <u>35</u> dollars.

> I like those <u>shoes</u>. How much are they?
> They're <u>50</u> dollars.

FURTHER PRACTICE (Wall Chart Set 1)

A. Talk about Age

*Have students ask each other about their age.

> S1: How old <u>are you?</u>
>
> S2: <u>I'm 24.</u>
>
> S1: How old <u>is she?</u>
>
> S2: <u>She's 18.</u>

B. Practice Making Comparisons

*Have students look at the beakers and compare fractions.

> S1: Which is <u>more—a quarter or a third?</u>
>
> S2: <u>A third is more than a quarter.</u>
>
> S1: Which is <u>less—a quarter or a third?</u>
>
> S2: <u>A quarter is less.</u>

C. Activity

*Play Bingo in English to help students practice understanding numbers said rapidly.

D. Discussion

**Ask students about things people do at different ages in their countries.

> T: In the U.S., people usually start going to school at 5. When do people start school in your country?
> When do people start dating?
> When do they get married?
> When do they join the army?
> When do they start working?
> When do they stop working (retire)?

TIME

PRIMARY OBJECTIVES

Tell time using both digital and analog time words.
Recognize and describe the times and activities on the page.
Recognize the difference between A.M. and P.M. and use each appropriately when telling
time.

CONVERSATIONAL OBJECTIVE

Tell what time students do various daily activities.

RELATED UNITS

Numbers (page 1), Action at Home (page 26)

CULTURAL COMMENTS

Attitudes and behavior regarding time vary tremendously in different cultures, particularly
in relation to such activities as mealtimes and worktimes.

- Although there are variations, people in North America generally eat breakfast
  some time between 6:00 and 9:00 A.M., lunch some time between 12:00 and 2:00
  P.M., and dinner some time between 6:00 and 8:00 P.M. On weekends, meals are
  usually an hour later.
- The normal workday in the U.S. is generally considered to last from 9:00 A.M. to
  5:00 P.M. Some people work from 8:00 A.M. to 4:00 P.M. or 10:00 A.M. to 6:00 P.M.
  People generally take between a half hour and an hour for lunch in the middle of
  the workday.
- Business appointments, business lunches, and job interviews are always meant to
  be exactly at the appointed time. It is considered rude to be late, even five minutes
  late. Social engagements have more flexibility. It is usually all right to arrive 10 or
  15 minutes late.

VOCABULARY NOTES

Alternate Words

E-watch = wristwatch

Additional Words

clockwise: indicates circular movement in the direction the hands of a clock move.
counterclockwise: indicates circular movement opposite the direction the hands of a clock
move.

RELATED IDIOMS AND EXPRESSIONS

to call time out: to stop an activity for a few minutes. Usually used in sports, games, or contests.

spare time: free time.

to have time on your hands: to have extra time with nothing to do.

overtime: more time than is scheduled or planned.

Time flies (when you're having fun): a stand-alone expression used to suggest that time is passing quickly (because you are enjoying yourself).

to have the time of your life: to enjoy yourself very much.

to tell time: to be able to read a clock.

MINI-PRACTICE NOTES

Alternate Structures

Introduce alternative ways of asking for the time.

> What's the time?
> Do you know the time?
> Do you have the time?
> Do you know what time it is?
> Could you tell me the time, please?

FURTHER PRACTICE (Wall Chart Set 1)

A. Talk about Telling Time

*Have students look at digital and analog watches and practice identifying alternative ways of telling time. Read a time two ways. Students say whether they are the same time or different.

> T: It's seven o five. It's five after seven.
> S: Same.
>
> T: It's seven fifteen. It's a quarter to seven.
> S: Different.
>
> T: It's seven fifty. It's a quarter after seven.
> S: Different.
>
> T: It's seven thirty. It's half past seven.
> S: Same.

B. Discussion

*1. Ask students what time they do their daily activities.

> T: What time do you get up?
> What time do you eat breakfast?
> When do you go to work?
> When do you leave for school?
> When do you eat lunch?
> What time do you eat dinner?
> When do you go to bed?

**2. Ask students to describe the activities of friends and family in their country at various times of the day.

> T: It's two o'clock in the afternoon. What's your mother doing?

S: She's cooking.

T: What's your father doing?

S: He's sleeping.

T: What's your sister doing?

S: She's walking the dog.

CALENDAR & HOLIDAYS   Page   3

PRIMARY OBJECTIVES

Recognize and name the months in chronological order.
Recognize and name the days of the week in chronological order.
Recognize and describe the meaning of the holidays on the page.

CONVERSATIONAL OBJECTIVES

Discuss students' likes and dislikes of particular holidays.
Talk about holidays in students' country and compare their holidays with those on the
  page.

RELATED UNITS

Numbers (page 1), **Weather & Seasons** (page 4), **The Family** (page 31)

CULTURAL COMMENTS

Some of the holidays on the page are celebrated universally. Others are celebrated mainly
  in the U.S.

Universal Holidays

New Year's Day: celebrates the start of a new year. Always on January 1.
Easter: Christian holiday celebrating the resurrection of Jesus Christ. The exact date of
  this holiday varies from year to year, but it is always on a Sunday in the spring.
Mother's Day: honors mothers and grandmothers. Always on the second Sunday in
  May.
Father's Day: honors fathers and grandfathers. Always on the third Sunday in June.
Christmas: Christian holiday celebrating the birth of Jesus Christ. Always on Decem-
  ber 25.

U.S. Holidays

Valentine's Day: a day when friends, lovers, and married couples exchange presents.
  Not a day off from work or school. Always celebrated on February 14.
Washington's Birthday: honors George Washington, America's first President. Always
  the third Monday in February.
St. Patrick's Day: honors all Irish and Irish-Americans. Not a day off from work or
  school. Always celebrated on March 17.

Memorial Day: honors Americans who died in wars for the United States. Always the last Monday in May.

Fourth of July: celebrates America's independence from England. Always celebrated on July 4th.

Labor Day: honors Americans who work by giving them a day off. Labor Day is a sign of the end of summer, and is always celebrated on the first Monday in September.

Halloween: a holiday when children dress up in costumes and go to neighbors' houses asking for candy. Not a day off from work or school. Always on October 31.

Thanksgiving: celebration of the Pilgrims' first harvest in North America. Always on the fourth Thursday in November.

April 1 is not a holiday, but is known as April Fool's Day. On this day, people play practical jokes on each other. When the person realizes he or she has been the victim of a practical joke, the joker usually yells "April Fool!"

Friday the 13th is recognized as a day of bad luck among the superstitious. Breaking a mirror, walking under a ladder, spilling salt, stepping on a crack in the sidewalk, and having a black cat cross your path are also superstitions that supposedly bring bad luck. Friday the 13th can be any Friday that comes on the 13th of the month.

Election Day is usually the first Tuesday in November. A national election for the President of the United States is held every four years on Election Day. State and local elections may be held on this date every year.

VOCABULARY NOTES

Usage

Most people exchange good wishes at each holiday. We usually say "Happy . . . (holiday name)" as in "Happy Valentine's Day." Note, however, that we generally say "Merry Christmas" rather than "Happy Christmas."

Xmas is a short form for *Christmas*, used more often in written than in spoken English.

Additional Words

Daily, weekly, monthly, and *yearly* are adjectives or adverbs used to describe events that occur every day, week, month, or year, respectively.

RELATED IDIOMS AND EXPRESSIONS

school day (SYN weekday): a day on which there is school.
school night (SYN weeknight): a night before a school day.
weekend: Saturday and Sunday.

MINI-PRACTICE NOTES

Usage

The date is written with the month first, then the day, then the year. This is true in both numerical and written form. People do not always include the year when writing the date. When we use the numerical form, we generally use only the last two numbers of the year. When we use the full written form, we generally write the whole year in numerical form.

Examples:
1/10/89 or January 10, 1989
2/21/43 or February 21, 1943
Years are pronounced as though they were two two-digit numbers: nineteen eighty-nine
  (1989).
Months are abbreviated in written English as follows: Jan., Feb., Mar., Apr., Jun., Jul.,
  Aug., Sept., Oct., Nov., Dec. *May* is never abbreviated.
The shortest abbreviations for the days of the week are shown on the page. They may also
  be abbreviated as follows: Sun., Mon., Tues., Wed., Thurs., Fri., Sat.

FURTHER PRACTICE (Wall Chart Set 2)

A. Practice with Ordinals

*Present the ordinal numbers from *first* to *thirty-first*. Have the students repeat after you,
  making sure they are able to distinguish the following pairs that sound similar: 20th/28th,
  20th/25th, 13th/30th, 22nd/27th.

B. Talk about Birthdays

*Have students ask each other about their birthdays.

> S1: When's your birthday?
>
> S2: November 28th.
>
> S1: What year were you born?
>
> S2: 1970.

C. Talk about Astrological Signs

*Expand the topic of birthdays. Copy the list below on the board and have students ask
  and answer questions about their astrological signs.

AQUARIUS: Jan. 21–Feb. 18	LEO: July 23–Aug. 22
PISCES: Feb 19–Mar. 20	VIRGO: Aug. 23–Sept. 22
ARIES: Mar. 21–Apr. 19	LIBRA: Sept. 23–Oct. 23
TAURUS: Apr. 20–May 20	SCORPIO: Oct. 24–Nov. 21
GEMINI: May 21–June 21	SAGITTARIUS: Nov. 22–Dec. 21
CANCER: June 22–July 22	CAPRICORN: Dec. 22–Jan. 20

> S1: When's your birthday?
>
> S2: August 15th.
>
> S1: Are you a Leo?
>
> S2: Yes, I am.
>
> S2: When's your birthday?
>
> S1: March 1st.
>
> S2: What's your sign?
>
> S1: Pisces.

D. Discussion

**1. Find out how many people in the class were born under the same sign. Ask the
  students if they think these people share similar characteristics.

**2. Ask students to talk about their favorite month of the year.

> T: What's your favorite month of the year?
> Why is it your favorite month?
> What do you like to do during that month?

**3. Ask students to talk about their favorite day of the week.

> T: What's your favorite day of the week?
> Why is it your favorite day?

**4. Have students look at the photos and describe as many details about each North American holiday as they can.

> T: What's the holiday?
> When is it?
> What do people do on this holiday?
> Do people eat anything special?
> Is there a holiday like this in your country?
> How is it different/the same?

Ordinal Numbers

first	ninth	seventeenth
second	tenth	eighteenth
third	eleventh	nineteenth
fourth	twelfth	twentieth
fifth	thirteenth	twenty-first
sixth	fourteenth	thirtieth
seventh	fifteenth	thirty-first
eighth	sixteenth	

WEATHER & SEASONS   Page   4

PRIMARY OBJECTIVES

Recognize and describe seasons and weather.
Recognize and distinguish between Celsius (Centigrade) and Fahrenheit temperature readings.

CONVERSATIONAL OBJECTIVES

Recognize and describe the seasons in relation to months of the year in the U.S. and other countries.
Talk about students' favorite and least favorite weather and seasons.
Talk about the activities students like to do in various seasons.

RELATED UNITS

Calendar & Holidays (page 3), **Men's Wear** (page 35), **Women's Wear** (page 36), **Men's & Women's Wear** (page 37), **The Beach** (page 62), **Water Sports** (page 63), **Winter Sports** (page 64), **Other Sports** (pages 67–68).

CULTURAL COMMENTS

In North America, the summer (warm weather) months are generally June, July, and August. The fall months are generally September, October, and November. The winter (cold weather) months are generally December, January, and February. The spring months are generally March, April, and May.

People often talk about the weather when they don't know what else to talk about, or when trying to initiate a conversation with a stranger.

The Celsius/Centigrade temperature scale is used in Canada and most of the rest of the world. Attempts are being made to introduce the use of the Celsius scale to the U.S., but the Fahrenheit scale is still used most frequently.

VOCABULARY NOTES

Usage

The following are alternate ways of describing weather:

5—It's a sunny day./The sun is out.
6—It's a rainy day./It's raining.
7—It's a snowy day./It's snowing
10—It's a cloudy day./There are lots of clouds in the sky.
12—It's a foggy day./There's lots of fog.
13—It's a windy day./There's lots of wind.

Additional Words

humidity: the amount of moisture in the air.
humid: moist, usually refers to the air or weather.
muggy: hot and humid.
storm: heavy rain (or snow) **and** fast winds.
hurricane: a severe storm with winds faster than 74 mph.

RELATED IDIOMS AND EXPRESSIONS

to pour (buckets): to rain heavily or hard.
to rain cats and dogs: to rain extremely heavily.
snowed in: trapped somewhere because of snow.

MINI-PRACTICE NOTES

Usage

In the example, the question asks if it is hot. Therefore, if students answer "yes," their answer must include a temperature between 85 and 105 degrees. If they answer "no," they must include a temperature in a different range. This exercise may be done with the Celsius scale, especially for use outside the U.S. For classes in the U.S., we suggest practicing with the Fahrenheit scale.

FURTHER PRACTICE (Wall Chart Set 1)

A. Talk about the Weather

*1. Ask students how they feel about different kinds of weather.

T: Do you like rainy days?
Do you like very hot days?
Do you like very cold days?

**2. Ask students how they feel about different kinds of weather and what they usually
do in that weather.

T: Do you like <u>rainy</u> days?

S: Yes, I do./No, I don't.

T: What do you usually do on <u>rainy</u> days?

S: <u>I go for long walks./I stay home.</u>

B. Talk about the Temperature

*Have students describe the weather using the Fahrenheit temperature scale.

T: It's <u>90</u> degrees.

S1: It's <u>hot.</u>

T: It's <u>40</u> degrees.

S2: It's <u>cold.</u>

C. Discussion

**Explain that in many parts ot the U.S. and Canada there are four seasons. Winter
usually includes December, January, February, March. Spring usually includes April,
May, June. Summer usually includes July and August. Fall usually includes September,
October, and November.
Ask students how many seasons there are in their country, when the seasons occur, and
which is their favorite season. Have students describe their favorite season.

SHAPES & MEASUREMENTS

Page 5

PRIMARY OBJECTIVES

Recognize and describe the shapes on the page.
Measure in feet and inches the shapes on the page.
Recognize and describe the number of inches in a foot.
Recognize and describe the number of feet in a yard.

CONVERSATIONAL OBJECTIVES

Recognize and describe the difference between the U.S. system of measurements and the
metric system.

Talk about objects in terms of their shape, size, and measurements.
Talk about the depth, width, length, and height of shapes.

RELATED UNIT

Numbers (page 1)

CULTURAL COMMENTS

Although the United States has tried to adapt to the more universal metric system, we still use the system of feet and inches rather than meters and centimeters.

VOCABULARY NOTES

Additional Words

Liquid Measures

one ounce = 29.5 ml
cup = 8 ounces = 236 ml
pint = 16 ounces = 473 ml
quart = two pints = 32 ounces = 946 ml
33.8 ounces = liter
gallon = 128 ounces = four quarts = 3.784 liters

Usage

Measurement words such as *depth, width, height,* and *length* are used as nouns. These words have adjective forms which are frequently used in measurement: *deep, wide, high,* and *long.* For example, we can say "What's the depth of the box?" or "How deep is the box?", "What's the width of the box?", or "How wide is the box?"

RELATED IDIOMS AND EXPRESSIONS

a *square*: someone who is considered unpopular or socially unknowledgeable.
a *vicious circle*: an argument that goes in circles rather than progressing logically from step to step.
squared away: solved, settled, or in order.

MINI-PRACTICE NOTES

Additional Structures

Introduce the following structures:

How deep is . . . ?
How long is . . . ?
How wide is . . . ?

Have students measure in feet and inches various objects in the classroom.

FURTHER PRACTICE (Wall Chart Set 2)

A. Talk about the Measurements

*Have students ask each other about their height. Students should express their height in feet and inches.

S1: How tall are you?

S2: I'm five feet six inches tall./I'm five six.

S2: How tall are you?

S1: I'm six feet one inch tall./I'm six one.

B. Activity: What Shape Is It?

*Divide the class into two teams. Have students look at the photos and ask each other to name as many objects as they can that illustrate the shapes on the chart. There are different correct answers. Any correct answer wins a point.

S1: Name something that's shaped like a circle.

S2: A clock/the moon.

S2: Name something that's shaped like an isosceles triangle.

S1: A hanger/a roof.

C. Activity: What Are the Measurements?

*Each student will need a ruler. (Students who do not have a ruler can make their own.) Divide the class into two teams, or students can work in pairs. Select six objects in the classroom. Have students measure the height, depth, length, width, and/or diameter of the six objects. The team that gets all the measurements correct wins.

D. Discussion

**Have students discuss their opinions about height. Explain that people from different cultures often have different ideas about people's height. In North America, for example, height is often associated with popularity and success.

T: Do people in your country think it's better to be tall or short?
Are you satisfied with your own height? Would you rather be taller or shorter?
What's the perfect height for a man?
What's the perfect height for a woman?
Women: Would you date a man who's shorter than you? Why?
Men: Would you date a woman who's taller than you? Why?
How tall would you want your son to be?
How tall would you want your daughter to be?

MONEY & BANKING

PRIMARY OBJECTIVES

Recognize and describe U.S. money and banking items.
Recognize and use numbers associated with money.
Make change for U.S. money.

CONVERSATIONAL OBJECTIVES

Talk about different forms of money (credit card, check, cash, etc.) and the different uses
    for each form.
Perform simple transactions at a bank.
Talk about attitudes toward money in different countries.

RELATED UNIT

Numbers (page 1)

CULTURAL COMMENTS

Denominations of U.S. currency: A penny is worth 1 cent; a nickel is worth 5 cents; a dime
    is worth 10 cents; a quarter is worth 25 cents; there are 100 cents in a dollar.
Fifty-cent pieces and silver dollars are very rarely used. You cannot use them in most
    vending machines. Pennies also are not used in vending machines.
Many people try to do their banking by mail or at the cash machine. Cash machines can
    perform most banking transactions, and are available 24 hours a day. If you want to
    buy money orders or traveler's checks, you usually must go to a teller.

VOCABULARY NOTES

Usage

Buck is slang for dollar.
We generally do not say "Do you have change for a one?" Instead, we say "Do you have
    change for a dollar?"
We generally do not say "Here are five one-dollar bills." Instead, we say "Here are five
    ones."
A vault is used to store valuable items like jewelry and important papers, such as insur-
    ance policies, stocks and bonds, and legal documents.
Amounts of money less than a dollar are followed by a cent (¢) sign: 10¢. Amounts
    greater than or equal to a dollar are preceded by a dollar ($) sign: $4.98.

Additional Words

change: collective noun used for pennies, nickels, dimes, and quarters. Also called *silver*.

RELATED IDIOMS AND EXPRESSIONS

You can bank on it: You can depend on it.
. . . and change: an unspecified amount less than a dollar.

MINI-PRACTICE NOTES

Alternate Structures

Break is another word for *change* when used as a verb in relation to money. The following two sentences are synonymous:

> "Can you change a five for me?"
> "Can you break a five for me?"

Introduce these structures as alternatives to the structure in the mini-practice.

A. Talk about Changing Money

*Have students ask each other to change money.

> S1: Can you change a <u>twenty</u> for me.?
>
> S2: Sure. Here are <u>four fives</u>.
>
> S2: Can you change a <u>fifty</u> for me?
>
> S1: Sure. Here are <u>two twenties and a ten</u>.

B. Discussion

**1. Explain that cash is currency, or paper money, as opposed to credit cards or checks. Ask students to describe the way people deal with money and banking in their country.

> T: Do many people have checking accounts in your country?
> Do people have to go to the bank to pay their bills, or can they pay by check?
> Do you have automatic tellers in your country?
> Do many people have savings accounts in your country?
> Do many people have credit cards in your country?

**2. Explain the values of the penny, nickel, dime, and quarter. Tell students that a nickel is larger in size than a dime, but a dime is worth twice as much. Have students describe the denominations of currency in their country.

> T: What's the largest bill in your country?
> What's the smallest bill in your country?
> What's the largest coin?
> What's the smallest coin?
> Are the bills all the same color?
> What color are the bills?

C. Role Play

**Have students take turns playing a bank teller and a customer buying traveler's checks or money orders. Students decide if the bank charges a commission; if the customer has to provide identification; and if the customer has to pay cash for the money order or if he or she can pay by check.

THE WORLD

PRIMARY OBJECTIVES

Recognize and name the countries of the world.
Recognize and describe the countries of the world by continent.
Recognize and name the major oceans and seas of the world.

CONVERSATIONAL OBJECTIVES

Talk about where students are from.
Talk about which countries of the world are alike.
Talk about countries students would like to visit.

RELATED UNITS

United States (page 9), Canada (page 10)

CULTURAL COMMENTS

People from the United States refer to themselves as Americans. It should be noted that people from Canada and Mexico may refer to themselves as North Americans. People from other parts of North and South America often feel insulted when people from the U.S. think they are the only ones who are Americans.

VOCABULARY NOTES

Alternate Words

the Netherlands = Holland
Russia = the Soviet Union

Usage

Great Britain is composed of three countries: England, Scotland, and Wales.
Central America is composed of seven countries: Guatemala, Belize, El Salvador, Honduras, Nicaragua, Costa Rica, and Panama.
The term *Latin America* generally refers to the countries of South America and Central America, Mexico, and the Spanish-speaking islands of the Caribbean.
Australia is both a country and a continent.

RELATED IDIOMS AND EXPRESSIONS

to go Dutch: to share a bill when on a date.
It's all Greek to me (SYN I can't make head or tails out of it): I don't understand any of it.

MINI-PRACTICE NOTES

Additional Structures

Use the mini-practice from pages 9 and 10 with the world.

> Is <u>Chile west of Argentina</u>?
> Yes, it is.
> Is <u>Mongolia south of China</u>?
> No, it isn't.

FURTHER PRACTICE

A. Talk about Where You Are From

*1. Have students ask each other where they are from.

> S1: Where are you from?
> S2: I'm from <u>Paraguay</u>.

*2. Have students ask each other where classmates are from.

> S1: Where's he from?
> S2: He's from <u>Japan</u>.
> S2: Where's she from?
> S1: She's from <u>France</u>.

B. Discussion

**Ask students about their travels.

> T: What countries have you visited?
> Have you ever lived in another country? Where?
> What things did you like or dislike about the countries you've visited? Why?
> What's your favorite country in the world? Why?
> What country would you most like to visit? Why?

C. Activity: Geography Game

**Students take turns naming a country or city anywhere in the world. Each student must name a country or city that starts with the last letter of the previous country or city. *Example:*

> S1: Brazil
> S2: Lebanon
> S3: Norway
> S4: Yugoslavia
> S5: Argentina
> S6: Afghanistan
> S7: New York
> S8: Kuwait
> S9: Togo
> S10: Oslo

If students cannot think of a country or city within a certain amount of time (10 seconds, for example), they are out of the game. Also, if a student repeats a country or city, he or she is out. The winner is the last student left in the game. The game may also be played in teams. Each time a team cannot think of a country or city, it loses a player.

D. Role Play

Have students take turns playing a travel agent and a customer arranging a vacation trip. The customers tell the travel agents how much they want to spend, where they want to go, and how long they will be traveling. The travel agents recommend several trips.

THE UNITED STATES Page 9

PRIMARY OBJECTIVES

Recognize and describe the U.S. states on the page.
Recognize and describe the geographical areas of the U.S.
Describe the locations of the states using *north, south, east,* and *west.*

CONVERSATIONAL OBJECTIVES

Talk about states students would like to visit and why.
Talk about differences among the states and between the U.S. and other countries.

RELATED UNITS

The World (page 7), Canada (page 10)

CULTURAL COMMENTS

Each state in the United States is almost like its own country. Each state has its own government and is fairly self-sufficient. However, all the states are subject to the laws of the federal government.

The capital of the United States is Washington, D.C. You cannot see Washington, D.C. on the map because it is not a state—it is a district. D.C. stands for District of Columbia. Washington is not a part of any state. It is located between Maryland and Virginia. The U.S. government is located in Washington, D.C., and the President lives there.

Each state has a capital city. The state governments are located in the capital cities of each state. The biggest city in a state is not always the capital. For example, the capital of New York is Albany, not New York City; the capital of California is Sacramento, not Los Angeles.

The states in the southern part of the United States are usually warm all year round. The states in the northern part of the United States are warm in summer and cold in winter.

The largest percentage of people in the United States live in the East. The smallest percentage of people live in the Midwest and Rocky Mountain States.

VOCABULARY NOTES

Usage

North, south, east, and *west* can be used as adverbs: I'm driving north on First Avenue.
   They can also be used as nouns: It's cold in the North.
The continental United States are the 48 states that are connected to each other. The newest
   states, Alaska and Hawaii, are not part of the continental United States, which is
   sometimes called the contiguous 48 states.

RELATED IDIOMS AND EXPRESSIONS

Ugly American: an American traveler who complains about the country he or she is traveling in, or refuses to adapt to foreign customs.
all-American: something that is classically American.
Southern belle: a woman from the South.

MINI-PRACTICE NOTES

Additional Structure

Introduce the verb *to border.* A state that borders another state is next to it. For example,
   Kansas borders Nebraska to the north, Oklahoma to the south, Colorado to the west,
   and Missouri to the east.

What states border Iowa?

South Dakota, Nebraska (to the west), Minnesota (to the north), Wisconsin, Illinois (to the
   east), and Missouri (to the south).

FURTHER PRACTICE (Wall Chart Set 2)

A. Talk about the United States

*Have students ask each other about various states they have visited or would like to visit.

   S1: Have you ever visited Texas?
   S2: Yes, I have.
   S1: Did you like it?
   S2: Yes, I did./No, I didn't.

   S2: Have you ever visited New Jersey?
   S1: No, I haven't.
   S2: Would you like to?
   S1: Yes, I would./No, I wouldn't.

B. Activity: What State Is It?

**Divide the class into two teams. One student from team A looks at the chart and de-
   scribes a state in terms of its location. A student from team B identifies the state.

   S1: It's east of Colorado, West of Missouri, north of Oklahoma, and south of Nebraska.
      What state is it?
   S2: It's Kansas.

C. Discussion

**1. Ask students to tell why they would like to visit a particular state in the U.S.
**2. Ask students to choose one state which they think is most different from their country. Students should describe the differences. They can mention geographical, people, and food differences.

CANADA   Page   10

PRIMARY OBJECTIVES

Recognize and describe the Canadian provinces.
Recognize and describe the locations of Canadian provinces.

CONVERSATIONAL OBJECTIVES

Talk about provinces students would like to visit and why. Talk about differences among the provinces and between Canada and other countries.

RELATED UNITS

The World (page 7), **The United States** (page 9)

CULTURAL COMMENTS

Canada is the second largest country in the world by size. It has a population of slightly more than 26 million people, or approximately one-tenth the number that the United States has.
Canada has two official languages: French and English. Many people speak both French and English in Canada. French is spoken predominantly in the province of Quebec. English is predominantly spoken in most other parts of Canada.
The capital of Canada is Ottawa, a city in Ontario.
Very few people live in the Yukon Territory because the weather is extremely cold there.
Many Canadians live in the United States and many Americans live in Canada. It is very easy for Americans and Canadians to cross the border between the two countries.

VOCABULARY NOTES

Additional Words

province: a province is like a state: a bounded area of land that has its own government and laws.
territory: an area of land that does not have its own government or laws.

RELATED IDIOMS AND EXPRESSIONS

Canadian doubles: a tennis game in which two players play against one person.

MINI-PRACTICE NOTES

Additional Structures

Introduce the noun *border.* A border is the dividing line or boundary between states, countries, or provinces. For example, many of the Canadian Provinces are on the American border of Canada. When two provinces, states, or countries are on opposite sides of a border, they are said to share a border.

> Does <u>Manitoba</u> share a border with <u>Ontario</u>?
> Yes, it does.

> Does <u>Quebec</u> share a border with <u>Saskatchewan</u>?
> No, it doesn't.

FURTHER PRACTICE (Wall Chart Set 2)

A. Talk about Canada

*Have students ask each other about various provinces they have visited or would like to visit.

> S1: Have you ever visited <u>Quebec</u>?
> S2: Yes, I have.
> S1: Did you like it?
> S2: Yes, I did./No, I didn't.

> S2: Have you ever visited <u>Quebec</u>?
> S1: No, I haven't.
> S2: Would you like to?
> S1: Yes, I would./No, I wouldn't.

B. Activity: What Province Is It?

**Divide the class into two teams. One student from team A looks at the chart and describes a province in terms of its location. A student from team B identifies the province.

> S1: It's <u>east of British Columbia, west of Saskatchewan, and south of the Northwest Territories</u>. What province is it?
> S2: It's <u>Alberta</u>.

C. Discussion

**1. Ask students to tell why they would like to visit a particular province in Canada.
**2. Ask students to choose one province which they think is most different from their country. Students should describe the differences. They can mention geographical, people, and food differences.

THE CITY

PRIMARY OBJECTIVES

Recognize and describe the items on the page associated with big cities.
Express preferences and city living.

CONVERSATIONAL OBJECTIVES

Talk about advantages and disadvantages of several methods of transportation in a city.
Give directions.
Describe the route students take to class.

RELATED UNITS

The World (page 7), **The United States** (page 9), **Canada** (page 10)

VOCABULARY NOTES

Alternate Words

      7—traffic light = stop light
    26—exit = door
    27—passenger = rider

Usage

St. is the abbreviation for *Street*. *Ave.* is the abbreviation of *Avenue*. *Rd.* is the abbreviation for *Road*. *Blvd.* is the abbreviation for *Boulevard*.
A block is the distance between two streets or avenues, and is used when giving directions: The bus stop is three blocks from here.
Downtown generally refers to the business and commercial center of a city.

RELATED IDIOMS AND EXPRESSIONS

to make a left/right (SYN to hang a left/right, slang): to turn left/right.
to go against the light (OPP with the light): to cross an intersection when the traffic light is red or the walk sign says WAIT or DON'T WALK.
bumper-to-bumper traffic: very severe traffic.
across the street: refers to something on the other side of the street.
to flag down: to cause a bus or taxi to stop by waving at the driver.

FURTHER PRACTICE

A. Talk about the City

*Have students ask each other about living in the city.

S1: Do you live in the city?

S2: Yes, I do.

S1: Do you like living in the city?

S2: Yes, I do./No, I don't.

S2: Do you live in the city?

S1: No, I don't.

S2: Would you like to live in the city?

S1: Yes, I would./No, I wouldn't.

B. Discussion

**Reproduce the following chart on the blackboard. Then ask students to fill it in. Decide as a class which is the best method of transportation for traveling in a big city.

Method	Advantages	Disadvantages
Car		
Bus		
Subway		
Taxi		
Walking		

C. Role Play

**Have students take turns asking each other for directions around the city.

S1: How do I get to the <u>bank?</u> (post office, supermarket, drug store, hospital, etc.)

S2: <u>Go straight for two blocks and then turn left</u>

D. Activity

Have students describe the route they take to get to English class. For example, "I take the number 6 bus from Main Street to Smith Street. Then I walk three blocks on Davis Avenue and turn left onto Williams Road."

THE SUPERMARKET   Page 13

PRIMARY OBJECTIVES

Recognize and describe the supermarket items on the page.
Express preferences among supermarket items.

CONVERSATIONAL OBJECTIVES

Talk about who does the shopping in students households.
Make a shopping list.
Talk about preparing a favorite dish.

RELATED UNITS

Fruit (page 15), **Vegetables** (page 16), **The Menu** (page 17), **Fast Foods & Snacks** (page 18)

CULTURAL COMMENTS

Most people in the United States shop in a supermarket. They usually go once a week and buy all their food for the week. Some people go to the supermarket several times a week and buy only a few things.

Most supermarkets sell many items that you cannot eat, called non-food items. These generally include kitchen and bathroom items like the ones on pages 25, 45, 46, and 49.

VOCABULARY NOTES

Usage

A frozen dinner is often called a TV dinner.

Bread is sold by the loaf: I need a loaf of bread.

Cookies and crackers are sold by the box or package: I need a package of cookies.

Butter and margarine are sold by the pound, stick or tub: I need two sticks of butter and a tub of margarine.

A supermarket is often called a grocery store.

Chicken is sold whole, as in photo 23, or in parts. When sold whole, it is called a roaster or a whole frying chicken. When sold in parts, it is called by the parts' names: drumsticks (legs), thighs, wings, and breasts.

Additional Words

shopping cart: the basket in which you place your groceries while shopping at a supermarket. See photo D.

aisle: the lane between stacks of food. Most supermarkets have at least six aisles.

dozen: group of twelve. Eggs are sold by the dozen.

six pack: a group of six cans or bottles packaged together. Usually refers to beer or soda.

RELATED IDIOMS AND EXPRESSIONS

Don't cry over spilled milk: Don't get upset about something you can't change.

to have egg on your face: to be embarrassed.

to egg on: to urge, taunt, or tease.

to butter up: to flatter in an attempt to gain a favor.

to bring home the bacon: to earn money for a household.

On sale: with a special, lower price.

MINI-PRACTICE NOTES

Additional Structure

Introduce the following structure:

Do we need any <u>eggs</u>?

Yes, we do./No, we don't.

Do we need any <u>meat</u>?
Yes, we do./No, we don't.

FURTHER PRACTICE (Wall Chart Set 2)

A. Talk about the Supermarket

*Have students ask each other if they like various frozen foods and dairy items on the chart.

> S1: Do you like *frozen vegetables*?
> S2: Yes, I do./No, I don't.
> S2: Do you like *yogurt*?
> S1: Yes, I do./No, I don't.

B. Discussion

*1. Have students talk about who does the shopping in their household.

> T: Who makes the shopping list?
> Who does the shopping?
> Who pays for it?
> Who carries the groceries home?
> Who puts the groceries away?

**2. Have students talk about what they like and dislike about going food shopping. Ask them if they prefer to shop in a large supermarket or in a small neighborhood store or a market. Have them tell why.

**3. Ask students to tell about an interesting, funny, or strange experience they had when shopping for food.

FURTHER PRACTICE (Wall Chart Set 2)

A. Talk about the Supermarket

*Have students ask each other if they like various foods on the chart.

> S1: Do you like <u>tuna fish</u>?
> S2: Yes, I do./No, I don't.
> S2: Do you like <u>macaroni</u>?
> S1: Yes, I do./No, I don't.

B. Discussion

*1. Ask students to write a shopping list of things they would buy at the supermarket. The list should include food for a week for one person, two people, or a family of three or more, depending on the students' situation. Have some students read their lists aloud. The class can discuss the similarities and differences among the lists.

**2. Have students tell how they might cook one of the meat items on the chart.
You may want to introduce such verbs as *fry, broil, bake,* and *microwave.*
Students can refer to **Vegetables** (page 16), **The Menu** (page 17), and **Fast Foods & Snacks** (page 18) for additional vocabulary.

FRUIT

PRIMARY OBJECTIVES

Recognize and describe the fruit on the page.
Talk about fruit in terms of size.

CONVERSATIONAL OBJECTIVES

Express preferences among fruits.
Talk about making a fruit salad.

RELATED UNITS

The Supermarket (page 13), Vegetables (page 16), The Menu (page 17), Fast Foods & Snacks
   (page 18)

CULTURAL COMMENTS

Fruit is sold at supermarkets in the United States, but many people prefer to buy their fruit
   at separate fruit and vegetable stands or stores because they believe the fruit at supermarkets is not very fresh. Some people plant fruit in gardens in their backyards and
   pick it themselves. Other people drive to farms in the countryside and buy their fruit
   there.

Fruit is better in the summer than in the winter in many parts of the United States. Many
   fruits, such as peaches, plums, watermelon, cantaloupes, raspberries, and papayas, are
   not easy to find during the winter, and are not very fresh or tasty even if you can find
   them. Most fruit must be grown in warm climates and shipped to other parts of the
   country.

Papayas, kiwis, and mangoes are rarely grown in the U.S. and are therefore expensive
   because they must be imported from other countries.

Many people in the United States like to eat fruit on top of a bowl of breakfast cereal, or
   as a dessert, sometimes served with ice cream.

VOCABULARY NOTES

Additional Words

seed: the part inside an apple, pear, grape, kiwi, papaya, watermelon, honeydew melon,
   or cantaloupe that you plant to grow more of the fruit.

pit or stone (or *pip* in some parts of the country): the part inside a mango, avocado,
   nectarine, plum, cherry, apricot, lemon, lime, grapefruit, orange, or peach that you plant
   to grow more of the fruit.

citrus fruits: lemons, limes, oranges, and grapefruits are called citrus fruits because they
   contain citric acid.

prune: a plum that has had the water dried out of it.

raisin: a grape that has had the water dried out of it.

melon: a general term for watermelons, cantaloupes, and honeydew melons.

RELATED IDIOMS AND EXPRESSIONS

to compare apples and oranges: to compare items that have little or nothing in common.
a bad apple (also, a bad egg): something that is bad in a group of otherwise good objects.
to be bananas/go bananas: to become crazy (slang).

MINI-PRACTICE NOTES

Usage

Most fruit is sold by the pound. There are exceptions, however. A group of bananas or
grapes is called a bunch, but each bunch must be weighed and sold by the pound.
Have students ask to buy fruit according to the way it is sold.

> I'd like a pound of apples.
> I'd like a bunch of grapes.

FURTHER PRACTICE (Wall Chart Set 1)

A. Talk about Fruit

*Ask students to talk about fruit in terms of size.

> T: Which is <u>bigger—a pear or a grape</u>?
> Which is <u>smaller—a lemon or a grapefruit</u>?

B. Practice with *a* and *an*

*Explain that words which begin with a vowel take the article an (an apple, an orange).
Words which begin with a consonant take the article a (a pear, a coconut).
Have students ask each other about their preferences.

> S1: Would you like <u>an apple</u>?
> S2: Yes, I would:/No, thanks. I'd rather have <u>a pear</u>.

C. Discussion

**Ask students questions about fruit.

> T: Which fruit do you like best?
> Which fruit do you dislike?
> Is there any fruit (on the chart) you've never tasted?
> Which fruit comes from your country?
> Do you eat fruit for breakfast? For dessert? For a snack?
> Do you cook with fruit?

D. Activity: Making a Fruit Salad

**Divide the class into two groups. Have each group write a recipe for an unusual or
special fruit salad. Ask one person in each group to read the recipe to the class. Have
the students choose the fruit salad they would most like to eat.
You might introduce terms such as: *mix, add, cut, peel, slice, stir, a cup of. . . .*
Students can refer to **Kitchenware** (page 46) for utensils associated
with these terms.

VEGETABLES

PRIMARY OBJECTIVES

Recognize and describe the vegetables on the page.
Categorize and describe vegetables by color and size.

CONVERSATIONAL OBJECTIVES

Express preferences among vegetables.
Make a shopping list for a vegetable dish.

RELATED UNITS

The Supermarket (page 13), Fruit (page 15), The Menu (page 17), Fast Foods & Snacks (page 18)

CULTURAL COMMENTS

See the Cultural Comments for Fruit (page 15).

VOCABULARY NOTES

Usage

Garlic, dill, and ginger are usually used as spices or garnishes—things that give additional flavor to other foods—rather than as foods themselves.
A single unit of celery is called a stick or stalk.
A single unit of asparagus is called a spear.

RELATED IDIOMS AND EXPRESSIONS

cool as a cucumber: very relaxed in a stressful situation.
carrot-top: person with red hair (slang).

MINI-PRACTICE NOTES

Additional Structure

Introduce the following structure. Note that the words that are listed in the singular on the page are collective, or mass, nouns.

How many tomatoes do we need?
Two.
How much celery do we need?
Two bunches.

FURTHER PRACTICE (Wall Chart Set 1)

A. Categorizing

*Have students look at the chart and categorize the vegetables by color, for example *Green/White/Yellow.*
Students can refer to "D. Colors" (pages 35 and 36).

B. Talk about Vegetables

*List the following vegetables on the board:

lettuce	tomatoes	cauliflower
potatoes	string beans	broccoli
corn	pearl onions	carrots
		cucumbers

Divide the class into two teams. Each team takes a turn describing one of the vegetables on the board. The other team must guess the name of the vegetable from the description.

Introduce words to describe the vegetables: *small, medium, large, orange, green, yellow, red, white, round, long, thin.*

TEAM A: It's large, round, and green.

TEAM B: It's lettuce.

TEAM B: It's long, thin, and orange.

TEAM A: It's a carrot.

C. Discussion

*1. Have students make a shopping list for their favorite recipe with vegetables. Encourage them to use the words *pound of, bunch of,* and *head of* in their lists.
**2. Ask students questions about vegetables.

> T: Which vegetables do you like best?
> Which vegetables do you dislike?
> Are there any vegetables on the page that you have never eaten?
> Which vegetables come from your country?
> Would you put vegetables in a salad?
> How often do you eat vegetables?
> Do you like cooked or uncooked vegetables?
> What's your favorite recipe for vegetables?

PRIMARY OBJECTIVES

Recognize and describe the foods on the page.
Express preferences among the foods on the page.

CONVERSATIONAL OBJECTIVES

Talk about typical menus in the U.S. and other countries.
Talk about eating in a restaurant.
Order a full meal.

RELATED UNITS

The Supermarket (page 13), Fruit (page 15), Vegetables (page 16), Fast Food & Snacks (page 18)

CULTURAL COMMENTS

People order their meals in a restaurant either complete or à la carte. A complete meal comes with an appetizer and soup or salad before the main course, and dessert and coffee after the main course. If you order à la carte, you order only the dishes you want.
Some people have a soup and a salad instead of a main course.
People usually drink water, milk, wine, coffee, or soft drinks with dinner. They drink coffee or tea after dinner.

VOCABULARY NOTES

Usage

Appetizers and soup and salad are often referred to collectively as first courses or starters.
Jello is a brand name of gelatin now used generically for all items of its type.
Meat is served many ways in the U.S. From least-cooked to most-cooked, they are: rare, medium rare, medium, medium-well, and well-done.
Decaffeinated coffee (decaf, for short) is coffee with little or no caffeine. Caffeine keeps some people awake at night or makes them nervous and tense.

RELATED IDIOMS AND EXPRESSIONS

a piece of cake (SYN easy as pie): very easy.
Soup's on: a slang expression meaning that dinner or lunch is ready.
It isn't my cup of tea: I don't like it.

MINI-PRACTICE NOTES

Alternate Structure

Introduce the following structure:

What would you like for your appetizer?
I'd like a shrimp cocktail.
What would you like for your main course?
I'd like roast beef with stuffed tomatoes.

FURTHER PRACTICE

A. Talk about the Menu

*Have students ask each other about the kinds of food they like and dislike.

S1: Do you like spaghetti and meatballs?

S2: Yes, I do./ No, I don't.
S2: Do you like chicken?

S1: Yes, I do./ No, I don't.

B. Discussion

**1. Ask students about eating in their country.

T: What kind of food do you eat for breakfast?
What kind of food do you eat for lunch?
What kind of food do you eat for dinner?
What's the biggest meal of the day in your country?
What time do you eat lunch in your country?
What time do you eat dinner in your country?
Do you eat any other meals besides breakfast, lunch, and dinner in your country?

Students may refer to **The Supermarket** (page 13-14), **Fruit** (page 15), and **Vegetables** (page 16) for additional vocabulary.

**2. Ask students about eating in restaurants.

T: How often do you eat in restaurants?
What kind of restaurant do you prefer?
What's the most popular kind of restaurant in your country?

C. Activity: Preparing a Menu

**Write a name of a fictional restaurant on the blackboard. Ask students to suggest items for the restaurant's menu. As students name dishes, ask them if the items are appetizers, soups, salads, main courses, beverages, or desserts. Then write them on the board until you have a full menu.

D. Role Play

*1. Have students take turns playing the waiter and a customer at a restaurant.
**2. Repeat Role Play 1 using the menu on the blackboard instead of the page.

PRIMARY OBJECTIVES

Recognize and describe the fast foods and snacks on the page.
Express preferences among fast foods and snacks.

CONVERSATIONAL OBJECTIVES

Talk about fast foods and snacks in other countries.
Talk about the couple in the center photo.

RELATED UNITS

The Supermarket (page 13), Fruit (page 15), Vegetables (page 16), The Menu (page 17)

CULTURAL COMMENTS

McDonalds, Kentucky Fried Chicken, and Burger King are American fast-food restaurants
which are well-known both in the U.S. and in many other countries.
People of all types and all ages eat fast food. They can sit down and eat in the restaurant,
or they can take the food out. The advantage of fast food is that it is cooked and ready
to go and people do not have to wait long to get it.

VOCABULARY NOTES

Alternate Words

1—hero/submarine sandwich has many geographical variants, including grinder,
hoagie, sub, poor boy (po-boy)
19—milk shake = frappe
20—soft drink = soda = pop = soda pop
24—hamburger = burger
25—hot dog = frank = frankfurter = wiener = weenie
27—french fries = fries = steak fries = french-fried potatoes

Usage

Pizza is often divided into slices and sold this way in fast-food restaurants. Chicken is often
divided into pieces and sold this way in fast-food restaurants.
Fast foods (items 1–5) generally replace a meal.
Snacks (items 11–20) are generally eaten between meals.
Condiments (items 6–10) are used to give flavor to foods.

RELATED IDIOMS AND EXPRESSIONS

take-out food (or take-out): food that you take out of the restaurant to eat. Take-out food is
usually fast food, but you can take out almost any kind of meal.
here, or to go: an expression used by clerks at fast-food restaurants. They want to know
whether you want to eat the food in the restaurant or if you want to take it with you.

MINI-PRACTICE NOTES

Additional Structure

Introduce the following structure (for taking and giving orders in fast-food restaurants):

> What would you like?
> I'd like a <u>hamburger</u>, please.

FURTHER PRACTICE (Wall Chart Set 1)

A. Talk about Fast Foods

*Ask students questions to practice using the words for condiments (items 6-10).

> T: What do you like on a <u>hamburger</u>?
> S: <u>Ketchup</u> and relish.
>
> T: What do you like on a <u>hot dog</u>?
> S: <u>Mustard</u> and <u>onions</u>.
>
> T: What do you like on a <u>hero</u>?
> S: <u>Mustard</u>.

B. Talk about Preferences

*Have students ask each other questions about their fast food and snack preferences.

> S1: Which do you like better—<u>hamburgers</u> or <u>hot dogs</u>?
> S2: Hot dogs.
> S2: Which do you like better—<u>popcorn</u> or <u>potato chips</u>?
> S1: Popcorn.

C. Discussion

*1. Ask students questions about fast foods and snacks.

> T: Do you like fast foods?
> What's your favorite fast food?
> When do you usually eat fast food?
> Do you like snacks?
> What's your favorite snack?
> Do you think snacks are good for you?
> When do you eat snacks?

**2. Have students talk about the couple in the center of the wall chart.

> T: Are they brother and sister?
> Are they on a date?
> Who is having the french fries?
> Who is having the onion rings?
> What are they talking about?
> Do young people in your community go alone to fast food restaurants?
> Do you think they are having a good time?

PRIMARY OBJECTIVES

Recognize and describe the post office objects and postal workers on the page.
Give students' address and zip code.

CONVERSATIONAL OBJECTIVES

Talk about postal service in the U.S. and other countries.
Talk about stamp collecting.

RELATED UNITS

The Office (page 20), Occupations (pages 21–22)

CULTURAL COMMENTS

It costs 25 cents to send a half-ounce letter anywhere in the United States.
The post office is run by the U.S. government.
When you send certified mail, the post office sends you a note (return receipt) that tells you when the letter has been received by the person you mailed it to.

VOCABULARY NOTES

Alternate Words

7—mail carrier = mailman = letter carrier = postman
17—zip code = zip (informal)

Usage

Mail is a word used to refer collectively to letters, postcards, and packages.
Mail is also used as a verb meaning "to send": I have to mail a letter.

MINI-PRACTICE NOTES

Usage

Another way of asking "What's your address" is to ask "Where do you live?" However, people may not give their full address if you ask them "Where do you live?"

FURTHER PRACTICE

A. Talk about Addresses

*Have students ask each other their address.

> S1: What's your address?
> S2: <u>420 Main Street.</u>

B. Discussion

**1. Ask students about the differences among various postal services.

> T: When do you use a mailbox instead of going to the post office?
> When do you go to the post office instead of using a mailbox?
> When do you send a postcard instead of a letter?
> When do you send a letter instead of a postcard?
> When do you send a certified letter?

**2. Ask students about stamp collecting.

> T: Do you collect stamps?
> When did you start collecting stamps?
> From what countries do you have stamps?

C. Role Play

**Have students take turns playing a customer and a postal clerk. The customer wants to mail a letter. The clerk asks whether he or she wants to send it regular mail, express mail, or certified mail. The customer asks how much each option costs and how long each takes. The clerk gives the customer the information. The customer decides, and pays the clerk.

THE OFFICE   Page   20

PRIMARY OBJECTIVES

Recognize and describe the office items on the page.
Recognize and describe the location of the items on the page using *in*, *on*, and *next to*.

CONVERSATIONAL OBJECTIVES

Talk about offices in other countries.
Express opinions about women working.
Talk about students' own jobs.

RELATED UNITS

The Post Office (page 19), **Occupations** (pages 21–22)

CULTURAL COMMENTS

A modern office might also contain a computer instead of or in addition to a typewriter. Secretaries can be male or female.

Some offices are more formal than others, which is reflected in the type of clothing worn by the staff.

VOCABULARY NOTES

Alternate Words

     4—pencil holder = pencil cup
    15—wastepaper basket = wastebasket = trash can

Usage

A switchboard is the telephone used by a receptionist and has many different phone lines accessible from the same instrument.

Xerox is a brand name for a photocopier used generically to refer to all items of its type. Xerox is also often used as a verb meaning "to photocopy."

Stationery refers to paper and envelopes used for writing letters. However, it may be used to refer to all items used in an office: pens, pencils, paper clips, note pads, tape, and file folders. A store that sells these items is called a stationery store or an office supplies store.

Additional Words

memo; memorandum: a short note sent by one person in an office to another person in the same office.

stenographer/typist: an office worker who types.

appointment: scheduled time to meet someone.

MINI-PRACTICE NOTES

Additional Structure

Introduce the plural form.

    Where are the staples?
    They're on the desk.
    Where are the paper clips?
    They're in the paper clip holder.

FURTHER PRACTICE (Wall Chart Set 2)

A. Talk about the Office

*Have students ask each other about working in an office.

    S1: Do you work in an office?

    S2: Yes, I do.

    S1: Do you like your job?

    S2: Yes, I do./No, I don't.

    S2: Do you work in an office?

    S1: No, I don't.

    S2: Would you like to?

    S1: Yes, I would./No, I wouldn't.

B. Activity: Debate

**Divide the class into two teams to debate the question: Should married women with children work? Each team is divided into two groups: a pro side and a con side. Appoint two judges in each group to decide which side has the better arguments. Have the judges summarize the conclusions for the class.

C. Role Play

**Have students play the role of a customer and a customer-service representative. The customer calls the representative to complain about a product.

D. Discussion

**1. Have students talk about the woman in the top photo. Students should give reasons for their opinions.

> T: Does this woman look like an executive or a secretary?
> Is her desk neat or messy?
> Is she well-dressed?
> Does she type?
> Do you think she's good at her job?
> Do you think she likes her job?
> Would you like this woman to work for you?
> Would you like to work for this woman?

**2. Ask students to talk about offices in their countries.

> T: Do most executives have offices?
> Are there any male secretaries?
> Are there any female executives?
> Do many married women work?

**3. Have students talk about their job (or the job they would like to have). They should describe the daily duties of this job as fully as possible and tell why they like (or would like to have) this job.

OCCUPATIONS   Page   21

PRIMARY OBJECTIVES

Recognize and describe the occupations on the page.
Practice with *a* and *an*.

CONVERSATIONAL OBJECTIVES

Talk about occupations held exclusively by men or by women.
Talk about knowledge of people in various occupations.

RELATED UNITS

The Post Office (page 19), **The Office** (page 20), **The Doctor** (page 29), **The Dentist** (page 30)

CULTURAL COMMENTS

The occupations in photos 24–31, 35, and 36 require a high level of education, usually
  several years of study after college at a professional school.
Sanitation workers, firefighters, police officers, and letter carriers are paid by the government. These occupations are often called civil service jobs.

VOCABULARY NOTES

Alternate Words

  31—pharmacist = druggist

Usage

A hairdresser and a barber both cut hair. Barbers generally cut men's hair, and hair-
  dressers generally cut women's hair.
A pediatrician is a doctor only for children. A doctor for adults is sometimes called a
  general practitioner or an internist.
A waiter and waitress perform the same jobs. A waiter is male and a waitress is female.
An optometrist prescribes glasses and contact lenses. An ophthalmologist is a doctor who
  treats diseases of the eye. An optician sells glasses and contact lenses.
Cop is a slang word for police officer.
There are many different kinds of artists: Painters, illustrators, sculptors, and musicians are
  the major types.

Additional Words

temp, or temporary worker: a person who works for a short time for different businesses or
  companies when they need extra help.
shift: a block of time, usually eight hours. Businesses that are open more than eight hours
  have their workers work in shifts. The graveyard shift is during the late-night and early-
  morning hours when most people are sleeping.

RELATED IDIOMS AND EXPRESSIONS

nine-to-five: refers to the hours that people generally work: from nine in the morning to
  five in the evening.
coffee break: a short period of time, usually 15 minutes, in the morning and afternoon
  when people stop work to have a cup of coffee or just relax.
tailor-made: perfect; as though made just for the occasion.

MINI-PRACTICE NOTES

Additional Structures

Introduce the following structure:

  Have you ever been a newscaster?
  Yes, I have./No, I haven't.

  Has your mother ever been a teacher?
  Yes, she has./No, she hasn't.

FURTHER PRACTICE (Wall Chart Set 1)

A. Talk about Occupations

*1. Have students ask and answer questions about their friends in various occupations.

    S1: Do you know any carpenters?
    S2: Yes, I do./No, I don't.

*2. Have students ask each other about their own occupations or professions.

    S1: Do you work?
    S2: Yes, I do.
    S1: What do you do?
    S2: I'm a waiter.
    S2: Do you work?
    S1: No, I don't.
    S2: What do you want to do?
    S1: I want to be a computer technician.

B. Discussion

**Ask students about the occupations of their close relatives (mother, father, husband, wife, sister, brother). Have students describe a relative who really likes his/her job or one who dislikes his/her job.

C. Activity: Name the Occupation

**Divide the class into two teams. One student on team A describes an occupation. One student on team B has to name that occupation.

    TEAM A: This person paints buildings.
    TEAM B: A painter.
    TEAM B: This person bakes bread.
    TEAM A: A baker.

FURTHER PRACTICE (Wall Chart Set 1)

A. Talk about Occupations

*Have students ask and answer questions about their friends in various occupations.

    S1: Do you know any secretaries?
    S2: Yes, I do./No, I don't.

B. Practice with *an*

*1. Have students look at the pictures and find the three occupations that can be preceded by *an* (optometrist, architect, and artist).

*2. Describe the work of various professions. Students guess the name of the occupation using *a* or *an*.

> T: She teaches school.
>
> S: A teacher.
>
> T: She draws pictures.
>
> S: An artist.
>
> T: He works in a bank.
>
> S: A teller.

C. Discussion

**1. Ask the students about men's and women's occupations in their country.

> T: Are there some occupations that are only for men?
> Are there some occupations that are only for women?
> Do you think men and women should have different occupations?

**2. Have students choose a picture and describe what is happening in the picture.

> S1: In number 24, a scientist is working. He's holding a test tube. He's in a laboratory.
>
> S2: In number 37, a secretary is talking on the telephone. She has a piece ot paper in her hand.

D. Role Play

**Have students play the role of a husband and a wife. The wife tells the husband that she wants to get a job, and that job would pay more money than his job. She asks what he thinks and he tells her.

THE BODY   Page   23

PRIMARY OBJECTIVE

Recognize and describe the parts of the body on the page.

CONVERSATIONAL OBJECTIVES

Talk about pain in different parts of the body.
Play Simon Says.

RELATED UNITS

The Doctor (page 29), Cosmetics & Toiletries (page 25), Action at Home (page 26), Action at the Gym (page 27).

CULTURAL COMMENTS

Redheads are more rare than blondes and brunettes.
There is no word for a person with black hair.
Many people dye their hair blonde because they think blondes are more attractive than brunettes. They believe the popular expression "blondes have more fun."

VOCABULARY NOTES

Alternate Words

> 17—nail = fingernail

Usage

Most people do not know the exact locations of items 51–61, which are collectively known as internal organs.
The plural of *tooth* is *teeth*.
A person who has little or no hair is bald.
The plural of *foot* is *feet*.
The plural of *calf* is *calves*.
Mustache is sometimes spelled *moustache*.
Hair can be either a singular (count) noun or a collective (mass) noun:

> My hair is brown. (collective, or mass, noun)
> There's a hair in my soup. (singular, or count, noun)

RELATED IDIOMS AND EXPRESSIONS

head and shoulders above (SYN *far and away better: a cut above*): much, much better.
at your fingertips: easily reachable or available.
on the other hand: alternatively, as an alternative.
to talk behind someone's back: to say bad things about someone who is not present. Opposite: say it to one's face.
to put your foot in your mouth: to say something innocently which ends up being embarrassing or harmful to yourself.
to cut off your nose to spite your face: to do something that will be harmful to someone else, even though it will be even more harmful to yourself.

MINI-PRACTICE NOTES

Additional Structure

Introduce the following structure.

> How many <u>knees</u> do you have?
> Two.
> How many <u>fingers</u> do you have?
> Ten.

FURTHER PRACTICE (Wall Chart Set 1)

A. Talk about the Body

*1. Call out the various commands for body movements and have students follow the commands.

> T: Open your eyes!
> Close your eyes!
> Touch your nose!
> Touch your head!
> Raise your arm!

**2. Increase the difficulty of these commands.

> T: Put your right hand on your left knee.
> Put your left hand on your right shoulder.

B. Activity: Simon Says

*Have students take turns, quickly giving commands to perform an action. The rest of the class performs the command only when the command is prefaced by the words "Simon Says." Anyone who performs a command when it is not prefaced by the words "Simon Says" is eliminated from the game. The last student left in the game is the winner.

> S: Simon says touch your <u>foot</u>.
>
> (Students touch their foot.)
> S: Simon Says touch your <u>nose</u>.
>
> (Students touch their nose.)
> S: Touch your <u>ear</u>.
>
> (Students are eliminated if they touch their ear. The other students continue playing the game.)

C. Role Play

Write some of the words and phrases for describing body pain on the board. Ask students to match these words with the numbers on the chart that indicate the body part. Students can refer to **"B. Sickness and Medicine" (page 29).

headache 24	broken arm 11	sore lip 7	sprained finger 15
earache 4	broken leg 18	sore eye 3	sprained foot 22
backache 26	broken ankle 35	sore knee 20	sprained wrist 13
stomachache 10			

Have students role play asking each other about their health, using appropriate body language and facial expressions.

> S1: How do you feel?
> S2: I have <u>a terrible headache</u>. (grimace, touch head)
> S1: <u>Oh, that's too bad</u>. (show sympathy and concern) I hope you feel better soon.
> S2: Thanks, I hope so, too.

Introduce other appropriate phrases for commenting on someone's pain, such as:

> *Gee, I'm sorry.*
> *What a shame!*
> *Oh, that's awful!*

COSMETICS & TOILETRIES

PRIMARY OBJECTIVES

Recognize and describe the cosmetics and toiletries on the page.
Describe actions performed with cosmetics and toiletries.

CONVERSATIONAL OBJECTIVES

Talk about what cosmetics and toiletries students use.
Talk about who wears cosmetics and why they wear it.
Discuss getting ready for a date.

RELATED UNITS

The Body (page 23), Action at Home (page 26)

CULTURAL COMMENTS

Most people in the U.S. take a shower every morning or every night. They are generally
very concerned about personal hygiene. People shower and use deodorant to cover their
body smells and mouthwash to cover mouth smells.
Cologne is for men or women. Perfume is stronger than cologne, and is used only by
women.
The brush in photo 21 is a men's brush. A women's brush is usually thinner.
The electric shaver in photo 23 is a men's shaver. A women's electric shaver is usually
thinner and comes in colors like white or pink. Women use electric shavers or razors to
shave their legs and under their arms.

VOCABULARY NOTES

Alternate Words

11—razor = safety razor
22—hair dryer = blow dryer
23—electric shaver = electric razor

Usage

An emery board is a nail file made of wood, rather than metal. The nail file in photo 18
is made of metal and is stronger and more durable than an emery board.

Additional Words

conditioner or cream rinse: a cream you put on your hair after shampoo.
deodorant or anti-perspirant: a toiletry you put on under your arms to prevent body odor.
makeup: a collective word for all cosmetics.

RELATED IDIOMS AND EXPRESSIONS

to have a brush with death: to nearly die.
to run a comb through: to comb quickly.
to brush off: to dismiss or send away; ignore
to brush up on: review or practice a skill.

MINI-PRACTICE NOTES

Usage

The following is a list of verbs used in relation to the toiletries on the page.

        9—wash (or shampoo) your hair
        10—shave
        15—comb your hair
        17—clip your nails
    18, 19—file your nails
        20—polish your nails
        21—brush your hair
        22—blow dry your hair

FURTHER PRACTICE

A. Talk About Cosmetics and Toiletries

*1. Have students ask each other, as appropriate, questions about the cosmetics and toiletries they use.

> S1: Do you use lipstick?
>
> S2: Yes, I do./No, I don't.
>
> S2: Do you use after shave?
>
> S1: Yes, I do./No, I don't.

**2. Have students ask each other what brands of cosmetics and toiletries they use.

> S1: What brand of shampoo do you use? (cologne, shaving cream, mascara, blush/rouge)
>
> S2: I use Revlon shampoo.
>
> S2: What brand of lipstick do you use?
>
> S1: I use Max Factor lipstick.

B. Discussion

**Ask students to discuss their feelings about cosmetics and toiletries.

> T: Why do you think people wear makeup, perfume, cologne, and/or after shave?
> Why do you think people wear nail polish?
> What cosmetics do you use and why?
> What cosmetics do people use in your country?
> Do people in the United States use more cosmetics than people in your country?

C. Activity: Getting Ready for a Date

**Reproduce the following chart on the blackboard:

Men		Women	
1.	6.	1.	6.
2.	7.	2.	7.
3.	8.	3.	8.
4.	9.	4.	9.
5.	10.	5.	10.

Ask the men in the class to name the first thing they do when they are getting ready for a date. Then ask the women to name the first thing they do when getting ready for a date. Then ask each group to name the second thing they do. Then the third thing, etc. Fill in the chart. Students should use vocabulary from the **Cosmetics & Toiletries** unit, but may also refer to **Action at Home** (page 26).

ACTION AT HOME   Page   26

PRIMARY OBJECTIVES

Recognize and describe the actions on the page.
Describe the things students do every day at home.

CONVERSATIONAL OBJECTIVES

Talk about who does the housework in students' homes.
Talk about what time they do daily routines.

RELATED UNITS

Cosmetics and Toiletries (page 25), **Action at the Gym** (page 27), **Action at School** (page 28).

CULTURAL COMMENTS

See the Cultural Comments from **Cosmetics & Toiletries** (page 25).

VOCABULARY NOTES

Usage

People often use *go to bed* and *go to sleep* interchangeably to mean "get into bed and begin sleeping."
Put some clothes on means "get dressed." *Throw some clothes on* means "get dressed quickly."
Jump in the shower means "take a shower quickly."
Cleaning the house usually includes dusting, sweeping, doing the laundry, and washing the dishes.
Listen is almost always followed by *to*: I like to listen to the radio.

RELATED IDIOMS AND EXPRESSIONS

to put someone to sleep: to cause someone to sleep.
Rise and shine: an expression used to wake somebody up, meaning "get up and start the new day."

MINI-PRACTICE NOTES

Additional Structure

Introduce the present continuous.

> What's the man doing (1)?
> He's waking up.
> What's the woman doing (8)?
> She's washing her face.

FURTHER PRACTICE (Wall Chart Set 1)

A. Practice with the Present Tense

*1. Ask students to name three things they usually do every day. Students can go beyond the language on the page.

> T: What do you do every day?
>
> S: I get up, take a shower, and get dressed.

*2. Play a memory game to practice the present tense with first and third person pronouns. The teacher begins with the question. Each student repeats what was said before and adds his or her own sentence. If a student cannot remember another student's activity, the student can ask that person "What do you usually do at night?"

> T: What do you usually do at night?
>
> S1: I cook dinner.
>
> S2: He cooks dinner and I eat dinner.
>
> S3: He cooks dinner, she eats dinner, and I listen to music.
>
> S4: He cooks dinner, she eats dinner, she listens to music, and I read.

B. Discussion

*1. Review ways of talking about time (see page 2). Ask students what time they usually do their daily activities.

> T: What time do you get up?
> What time do you eat breakfast?
> What time do you eat dinner?
> What time do you go to bed?

**2. Ask students to talk about who does the household chores in their homes, and in their country generally.

> T: Who cooks, sweeps, and dusts in your house?
> Do children usually help cook and clean the house in your country? Do men? Do women?
> Some people find cooking and cleaning relaxing and fun. Do you?

PRIMARY OBJECTIVES

Recognize and describe the actions on the page.
Practice with the simple present and present progressive.

CONVERSATIONAL OBJECTIVES

Talk about exercise habits.
Use the words on the page to practice calisthenics.

RELATED UNITS

Action at Home (page 26), **Action at School** (page 28), **Winter Sports** (page 64), **Spectator Sports** (page 65), **Other Sports** (page 67).

CULTURAL COMMENTS

Americans practice these actions to lose weight or to keep their bodies in good physical condition. It is important to many Americans to remain thin and in good physical shape.

VOCABULARY NOTES

Additional Words

to jump: to push yourself off the ground using both feet to spring into the air.
fitness; physical fitness: physical health or condition.
fit; physically fit (SYN in good shape): in good physical condition.

RELATED IDIOMS AND EXPRESSIONS

to stretch the truth: to exaggerate.
to reach for the stars: to try to excel.
to lift a finger: to make an effort to help.
to pull someone's leg: to lie, trick someone, or exaggerate.
to work out: to do exercise or lift weights.

MINI-PRACTICE NOTES

Usage

Introduce the past tense:
Have students pantomine the actions on the page.

> What did you do?
> I <u>ran</u>.

IRREGULAR PAST TENSE FORMS

1-bent	8-ran
3-sat	9-swung
4-lay down	11-caught
5-knelt	12-threw
7-hopped	

FURTHER PRACTICE (Wall Chart Set 1)

A. Practice with the Present Continuous

*Choose one student to pantomine an action in front of the class. Ask students to identify the action.

> T: What's he doing?
>
> S1: He's stretching.
>
> T: What's he doing now?
>
> S2: He's hopping.

Ask another student to continue the pantomime.

> T: What's she doing?
>
> S2: She's kneeling.

B. Practice with the Habitual Present

*Have students ask each other which activities they do every day.

> S1: What do you do every day?
>
> S2: I run every day.

C. Activity: Calisthenics

*Conduct a calisthenics class for about five minutes. Give students commands to bend, stretch, hop in place, run in place. Count each action.

> T: Bend and touch your toes—1,2,3,4.
> Stretch both arms—1,2,3,4.
> Bend to your left side—1,2,3,4.
> Bend to your right side—1,2,3,4.
> Run in place—1,2,3,4,5,6,7,8,9,10.
> Stretch both arms—1,2,3,4.
> Hop in place—1,2,3,4,5,6,7,8,9,10.

D. Discussion

**Ask students about their exercise habits.

> T: Do you get enough exercise?
> How often do you exercise?
> Do you like to exercise?
> Do you go to a gym now? Have you ever been to one? Describe it.
> Do you lift weights? Do you job? Do you do stretching exercises?
> Are there any actions on the chart you can't do?

PRIMARY OBJECTIVES

Recognize and describe the actions on the page.
Practice with the verbs on the page in the present progressive.

CONVERSATIONAL OBJECTIVES

Play charades.
Describe the actions in the photos in detail.
Express opinions about the people in the photos.

RELATED UNITS

Action at Home (page 26), Action at the Gym (page 27)

CULTURAL COMMENTS

Children in the United States must go to school until they are 16 years old. There are
   public schools, which are sponsored by state and local governments and are free, and
   private schools, in which parents pay for their children to attend.
It is considered impolite to point at someone in public.
The students in the photos are in high school and are dressed like typical U.S. high school
   students. Most high school students wear jeans and casual clothes. In some private
   schools, students must wear uniforms.

VOCABULARY NOTES

Alternate Words

     6—tear up = rip up
    23—fall = fall down

Additional Words

to put down: the opposite of to pick up. When the direct object is a pronoun, it goes
   between the words of these two-word verbs, rather than after them. When the direct
   object is a noun, it can go between the words of these two-word verbs or after these
   two-word verbs. Tear up is also a two-word verb and follows this same pattern.

    Put the book down or Put down the book.
    Now pick it up.

to get up: the opposite of to fall or fall down. Get up, go up, fall down, and go down do not
   follow the pattern described above. The direct objects used with these verbs are rarely
   pronouns, and are never placed between the two words.

    I couldn't get up after I fell down the stairs.

RELATED IDIOMS AND EXPRESSIONS

give and take: compromise.
to *cut short*: to end sooner than planned.
to *keep in touch*: to stay in contact with someone by letter or phone.
to *point a finger at*: to blame.
to *point out*: to call attention to.

MINI-PRACTICE NOTES

Additional Structures

Introduce the past tense.

What did you do yesterday?
I wrote a letter.

IRREGULAR PAST TENSE FORMS

1—wrote	12—cut
2—taught	13—drew
4—gave	19—went up
5—took	21—stood
6—tore up	22—went down
8—read (pronounced *red*)	23—fell down
9—picked up	

FURTHER PRACTICE (Wall Chart Set 1)

A. Practice with the Present Continuous

*Choose a student to pantomine an action from items 14–18 in front of the class. Pairs of students ask and answer questions about each action. The activity should be done rapidly—changing students and expressions often.

S1: What's she doing?

S2: She's frowning.

S2: What's he doing?

S1: He's smiling.

B. Activity: Charades

*Divide the class into two teams. One person on each team pantomines an action from the chart. The other team must guess the action within one minute.

C. Discussion

**Ask students to describe each scene in the chart. More advanced students can make up more inferential statements. There are four scenes: the classroom, the art room, the locker room, and the stairway.

T: Where's the teacher?
What are the students doing?
Are they happy?

Are they learning?
Are they all friends?
Do they know each other?
Are students in your country different in high school?
Do they dress differently?
Do they behave differently?

THE DOCTOR   Page 29

PRIMARY OBJECTIVES

Recognize and describe the sicknesses, medicines, and doctor's-office items on the page.
Diagnose simple illnesses and recommend simple remedies.

CONVERSATIONAL OBJECTIVES

Talk about personal experience with sickness and doctors.
Talk about doctors and health care in other countries.

RELATED UNITS

The Body (page 23), The Dentist (p. 30)

CULTURAL COMMENTS

People generally go to a doctor about once a year for an annual physical examination, or
    checkup, even if they feel healthy.
Doctors are very expensive in the United States. In some other countries, medicine is
    socialized, which means that the government pays the bill when you go to the doctor. In
    the United States, medicine is not socialized. However, many people join health-
    insurance programs. They pay an annual fee rather than paying each time they go to
    the doctor.
People do not generally go to a doctor for the sicknesses on the page. The medicines on
    the page are generally available in pharmacies or drug stores without a prescription
    from a doctor.

VOCABULARY NOTES

Alternate Words

    8—doctor = physician
    B—sickness = illness
    18—cough drops = cough tablets = lozenges

Usage

Band-Aid is a brand name used generically for all items of its type.

Cold tablets, cough syrup, and cough drops are often referred to collectively as cough medicine.

A general practitioner is a physician you go to for checkups, or physicals, and routine sicknesses. If you have a serious sickness, your physician will send you to a specialist who treats only specific illnesses.

Additional Words

hospital: a large building where you go when you have a serious illness or need surgery. Hospitals also provide health care in emergencies like accidents.

ambulance: a car or van that takes sick or injured people to a hospital as quickly as possible.

sick: not well.

healthy: the opposite of *sick*.

drug: a medicine or remedy for an illness.

RELATED IDIOMS AND EXPRESSIONS

to catch cold, or *to catch a cold:* to become sick with a cold.

in perfect health: healthy.

to be in pain: to have a pain.

over the counter: refers to medicine or drugs that you can buy without a doctor's prescription.

house call: when a doctor comes to your house because you are unable to go to his or her office.

MINI-PRACTICE NOTES

Additional Structure

Introduce the following structure:

> Do you have headaches often?
> Yes, I do./No, I don't.

FURTHER PRACTICE (Wall Chart Set 2)

A. Talk about Being Sick

*Have students ask and answer questions about photos 9–26.

> S1: What's wrong with her?
> S2: She has a headache.
> S1: What should she do?
> S2: She should take an aspirin.
>
> S2: What's wrong with him?
> S1: He has a cut.
> S2: What should he do?
> S1: He should use a Band-Aid.

B. Role Play

**Have students pretend they are in a doctor's office. One student takes the role of the doctor. The other takes the role of the patient. The doctor asks the patient about his/her problem. The patient responds. The doctor tells the patient what to do.
Students can refer to **The Body** (page 23) for additional vocabulary.

C. Discussion

**1. Ask the students about their health.

> T: How often do you go to the doctor?
> How often do you get sick?
> Do you ever get headaches?
> Do you often get colds?
> What do you do when you get a stomachache?

**2. Have students describe their doctor.

> T: What's your doctor like?
> Is your doctor a man or a woman?
> Is your doctor young or old?
> Is his/her office big or small?
> Does he/she work with other doctors or alone?
> Will your doctor come to your house when you're sick?
> Do you like your doctor?

THE DENTIST   Page   30

PRIMARY OBJECTIVES

Recognize and describe the dental items on the page.
Talk about personal preferences among dental hygiene products and habits.

CONVERSATIONAL OBJECTIVES

Talk about personal experiences in a dentist's office.
Talk about going to the dentist in other countries.

RELATED UNIT

The Doctor (page 29)

CULTURAL COMMENTS

Most Americans go to the dentist about once a year for a checkup and to have their teeth
cleaned. They also go to the dentist when their teeth or gums hurt.
Americans generally brush their teeth twice or three times a day.

VOCABULARY NOTES

Usage

floss is another word for *dental floss* when used as a noun. Both *floss* and *dental floss* are
collective nouns. Used as a verb, *to floss* means "to use dental floss."
Brush is another word for *toothbrush*. *To brush* is a short way of saying "to brush your
teeth."

Additional Words

cavity: a hole in your tooth caused by decay.
toothache: a pain in your teeth or gums.
needle (or hypodermic needle): device used to inject medicine or Novocain into your body
or mouth.

RELATED IDIOMS AND EXPRESSIONS

Open wide: the dentist tells you to do this when he or she wants you to open your mouth
as much as you can.
by the skin of your teeth: barely; only just
to lose a tooth: to have a tooth fall out of your mouth.
sweet tooth: an uncontrollable desire for sweet foods.

MINI-PRACTICE NOTES

Additional Structure

Introduce the following structure to practice *always*, *sometimes*, and *never*:

Do you ever use <u>mouthwash?</u>
No, I never do.
Do you ever use <u>a WaterPik?</u>
Yes, I sometimes do.

FURTHER PRACTICE (Wall Charts Set 2)

A. Talk about Your Teeth

*Have students ask and answer questions about their teeth.

S1: Do you <u>brush your teeth twice a day?</u>
S2: Yes, I do./No, I don't.
S2: Do you <u>use dental floss?</u>
S1: Yes, I do./No, I don't.

B. Role Play

**Have students pretend they are in a dentist's office. One student takes the role of the
dentist. The other takes the role of the patient. The patient tells the dentist the problem,
and the dentist tells the patient what he/she is going to do to help.

C. Discussion

**1. Ask students to talk about their experiences with the dentist.

> T: How often do you go to the dentist?
> Is your dentist a man or a woman?
> Does your dentist have a dental asistant?
> Does your dentist always give you Novocaine?
> Why do dentists use Novocaine?
> Do you always want your dentist to use Novocaine?
> Is it expensive to go to the dentist?
> Do you like your dentist?

**2. Divide the class into small groups. Have the students talk about a personal experience they had at the dentist's office. They should tell what the problem was, what the dentist did, and how they felt.

Students can refer to **Emotions** (page 32) for additional vocabulary.

THE FAMILY   Page 31

PRIMARY OBJECTIVES

Recognize and describe family members and relationships among them.
Use possessive pronouns.

CONVERSATIONAL OBJECTIVES

Talk about family members and relationships in students' families.
Talk about things students do with their families.
Talk about students' feelings toward some of their relatives.

RELATED UNITS

Emotions (page 32)

CULTURAL COMMENTS

Most children live at home with their parents until they are about 21 years old.
About one-third of all grandparents live with their children and grandchildren. And more than two-thirds of the people in the United States live in the same state as their parents.

Vocabulary Notes

Usage

The nuclear family usually consists of the parents and children in a family. The extended family consists of all the other relatives. For example, the members of Robert Shriver's nuclear family are Eunice Kennedy, Sargent Shriver, and his sister, Maria Shriver. The members of his extended family are all the people on the page.

People usually gather with their extended family during holidays like Christmas and Thanksgiving, when they have family parties and big dinners. These gatherings are usually called family times or family gatherings.

Mom, Ma, Mama, and Mommy are informal alternatives used by children when talking to or about their mother. People often continue to call their mother Ma or Mom when they are adults.

Dad, Pop, Papa, Pops, and Daddy are informal alternatives used by children when talking to or about their father. People often continue to call their father Dad or Pop when they are adults.

Grandma and Grandpa are informal alternatives children use when talking to their grandmother and grandfather.

People usually address their aunts and uncles by their first names, preceded by Aunt or Uncle. For example, Kathleen Kennedy would probably address Eunice and Sargent Shriver as Aunt Eunice and Uncle Sargent.

RELATED IDIOMS AND EXPRESSIONS

In-laws is a collective word used to describe your mother-in-law and father-in-law. It is not usually used to describe sisters-in-law or brothers-in-law.

Blood is thicker than water: an expression used to suggest that people in your family are more important and loyal to you than friends or strangers.

MINI-PRACTICE NOTES

Additional Structure

People have more than one relationship in a family. Have students describe the various relationships of one person on the page.

Rose is Joseph's wife, John's mother, and Caroline's grandmother.

A. Talk about the Family

*Have students ask each other about their families.

S1: How many brothers and sisters do you have?

S2: I have three brothers and two sisters.

S2: How many children do you have?

S1: I have four children: two boys and two girls.

B. Practice with Pronouns

*Have students use possessive pronouns instead of proper names in talking about the family.

S1: Who's Joseph's wife?

S2: Rose is his wife.

S2: Who's Caroline's father?

S1: John is her father.

C. Discussion

**Ask students about their families.

T: How many brothers and sisters do you have?
How many children do you have?
Do you want to have many children?
Do you live with your parents?
Do you spend a lot of time with your family?
Do people in the United States spend as much time with their family as people do in your country?

EMOTIONS   Page 32

PRIMARY OBJECTIVE

Recognize and describe the emotions on the page.

CONVERSATIONAL OBJECTIVES

Describe how students feel, using the list of emotions on the page.
Talk about a time when students felt certain emotions.

VOCABULARY NOTES

Alternate Words

1—pleased = glad
5—shocked = amazed = astounded
6—sad = unhappy
9—displeased = upset
22—shy = bashful

Usage

People often bite their nails when they are nervous.
People often yawn when they are bored or tired.
People often cry when they are sad, miserable, or grieving.
People often yell when they are mad or furious.

Additional Words

mood: a word similar in meaning to *emotion*. It is a state of expressing one's emotions. If you are in a good mood, you are usually pleased, happy, or ecstatic. If you are in a bad mood, you are usually sad, angry, annoyed, or bored.
depressed: a combination of sad, upset, and worried.

RELATED IDIOMS AND EXPRESSIONS

Down in the dumps: sad.
to chicken out (slang): to avoid something because you are afraid.
a worry wart: someone who worries too much.
dead set on: determined.
to smell a rat: to be suspicious.
to have your nose in the air: to think you are more important than everybody else.
to jump for joy: to be ecstatic.

The following expressions are more descriptive or expressive ways of talking about emotions:
as pleased as punch
as happy as a clam
scared to death
bored stiff
as proud as a peacock

FURTHER PRACTICE (Wall Chart Set 1)

A. Talk about Emotions

*Have students ask each other about how they really feel.

> S1: Are you <u>happy</u>?
> S2: Yes, I am./No, I'm not, I'm <u>bored</u>.

B. Play with Emotions

*Divide the class into two teams. One person on each team pantomimes an emotion agreed upon by the team. Players on the other team try to guess the emotion.

A student from Team A pantomimes "*confused.*"

> TEAM B: Is she <u>shy</u>?
> TEAM A: No, she isn't.

The student tries again.

> TEAM B: Is she <u>confused</u>?
> TEAM A: Yes, she is.

A student from Team B pantomimes an emotion.

C. Discussion

**Ask students to talk about a time when they were particularly *proud, furious, embarrassed, determined,* or *afraid.*

> T: What happened?
> When was that?
> Why did you feel that way?
> What did you do?

PRIMARY OBJECTIVES

Recognize and use the opposites on the pages.
Recognize and use comparative adjectives.
Recognize and use superlative adjectives.

CONVERSATIONAL OBJECTIVES

Discuss objects that illustrate the adjectives on the pages.
Talk about personal experiences, using superlatives.

RELATED UNITS

This unit will likely be used with almost every other unit in the book.

VOCABULARY NOTES

Alternate Words

        25—fast = quick
        38—crooked = bent
    47/48—over/under = above/below

Usage

Warm is not quite as hot as hot. Cool is not quite as cold as cold. It might be useful to
    refer back to **Weather & Seasons** (page 4) to review these terms.
neat/messy and *clean/dirty* are often used interchangeably.
Slim and *slender* are synonyms of *thin* when referring to people. If someone is too thin, he
    or she is skinny.

Additional Words

big and little: A basketball is big; a tennis ball is little.
large and small: see *big* and *little*. These sets of words are often used interchangeably.
fat and thin: a man who weighs 400 pounds is fat; a man who weighs 100 pounds is
    thin.
strong and weak: someone who can lift 400 pounds is strong; someone who can't lift 50
    pounds is weak.
rich and poor: someone who has $4 million is rich; someone who has $4 is poor.
cheap and expensive: a hamburger that costs $1 is cheap; a hamburger that costs $100 is
    expensive.

RELATED IDIOMS AND EXPRESSIONS

the long and short of it: the basic point.
hard and fast: rigid, immutable.

a long drink of water: a tall person
a spring chicken: a young person

The following expressions are similes—comparisons that use *like* or *as*. They are more expressive ways of using adjectives and are commonly used in spoken English.

as *light as a feather*	as *pretty as a picture*
as *ugly as sin*	as *dry as a bone*
as *straight as a stick*	as *slow as molasses*
as *old as the hills*	as *hard as a rock*
as *smooth as silk*	as *neat as a pin*

MINI-PRACTICE NOTES

Additional Structure

Continue the structure from the mini-practice, asking students to use examples from real life. Be sure students answer using the appropriate pronoun and form of the verb *to be.*

Are you <u>weak</u> or <u>strong</u>?
I'm <u>weak</u>./I'm <u>strong</u>.
Is your car <u>fast</u> or <u>slow</u>?
It's <u>slow</u>./It's <u>fast</u>.

FURTHER PRACTICE (Wall Chart Set 1)

A. Talk about Opposites

*Ask students to quickly tell you the opposite of words.

 T: What's the opposite of <u>young</u>?

 S1: <u>Old.</u>

 T: What's the opposite of <u>tall</u>?

 S2: <u>Short.</u>

B. Practice with Comparatives

**Introduce the regular comparative forms of the adjectives on this chart (*neater, messier, higher, lower, looser, tighter, lighter, heavier, longer, shorter, taller, younger, older, cleaner, dirtier, straighter, curlier, prettier, uglier*). Have students answer yes/no questions using the comparative.

 S1: Is <u>Lee</u> older than <u>Kim</u>?
 S2: Yes, he is.
 S1: Is a <u>book</u> heavier than a <u>TV</u>?
 S2: No, it isn't.

C. Practice with Superlatives

**Discuss the superlative form of the adjectives on this chart (*neatest, messiest, highest, lowest, loosest, tightest*, etc. Be sure to note the irregular forms *best* and *worst*). Ask students questions about their experiences.

 T: What's the messiest food you've ever eaten?
 What's the dirtiest job you've ever had?

Where's the wettest place you've ever visited?
What's the longest book you've ever read?
What's the worst movie you've ever seen?
What's the highest mountain you've ever seen?

FURTHER PRACTICE (Wall Chart Set 1)

A. Talk about Opposites

*Have students look at the pictures and ask each other to name as many objects as they can which illustrate the adjectives on the page.

> S1: Name something that is <u>hot</u>.
>
> S2: <u>Soup/tea/coffee</u>.
>
> S2: Name something that is <u>cold</u>.
>
> S1: <u>Ice/ice cream</u>.

B. Practice Making Comparisons

**Introduce the -er comparative form of the adjectives on this page (*faster, slower, hotter, colder, newer, older, lighter, darker, wider, narrower, thicker, thinner, softer, harder, smoother, rougher*).
Have students ask and answer *yes/no* questions using the comparative.

> S1: Is a plane faster than a <u>train</u>?
>
> S2: Yes, it is.
>
> S2: Is silk rougher than <u>wool</u>?
>
> S1: No, it isn't.

MEN'S WEAR   Page   35

PRIMARY OBJECTIVES

Recognize and describe the men's clothing on the page.
Talk about the clothes students have.

CONVERSATIONAL OBJECTIVES

Discuss favorite colors, patterns, and clothes.
Discuss appropriate clothes for certain situations.
Describe the appearance of other people in the class.

RELATED UNITS

Women's Wear (page 36), Men's & Women's Wear (page 37), Accessories (page 38)

CULTURAL COMMENTS

DRESS CODES. A dress code is the recommended or required style of dress for a particular event. There are several styles:

Formal, or black tie: men must wear a formal black dinner suit called a tuxedo and a black tie.

Informal, or coat and tie: men should wear a suit or a sportcoat and a tie.

Casual, or come as you are: No dress code. Men should wear jeans or casual clothes, though they may wear a sportcoat.

Men who work in offices generally wear a sportcoat, or suit and tie.

Men's shirts have either short sleeves or long sleeves. Short sleeves are considered more casual.

Men's suits are usually solid or have thin stripes called pinstripes and are usually a dark color like dark gray or dark blue. However, during summer, men often wear tan, light blue, or light gray suits.

VOCABULARY NOTES

Alternate Words

7—tie = necktie
9—sport coat = sportscoat
12—slacks = pants = trousers
17—boxer shorts = boxers
30—solid = plain

Usage

A shade is a variety of a color. The shades of blue include baby blue, light blue, navy blue, and royal blue.

Socks are referred to in the plural: I need to buy socks. They are also sold in pairs: I bought a pair of socks.

The shirt in photo 5 is often called a dress shirt to avoid confusion with a sport shirt (photo 13).

A suit with a vest is often called a three-piece suit.

The socks in photo 19 are dress socks. Sweatsocks are white and are worn with casual wear or athletic clothing.

Jockey shorts is a brand name which is used generically for all items of their type.

RELATED IDIOMS AND EXPRESSIONS

Shades of gray: used when there are many possible right answers to the same problem.
a white lie: a lie told to avoid hurting someone's feelings.
green with envy: very envious or jealous.
Below the belt: refers to an unfair or uncalled-for comment or blow.

MINI-PRACTICE NOTES

Additional Structures

Have students describe the items in the photos as fully as possible.

What's this (3)?
It's a gray striped suit.
What are these (17)?
They're solid blue boxer shorts.

Introduce the structure from **Women's Wear** (page 36).

What's he wearing (13)?
He's wearing a red plaid shirt.

FURTHER PRACTICE (Wall Chart Set 2)

A. Talk about Colors

*Have students ask each other about their favorite color.

S1: What's your favorite color?

S2: Blue.

Students can refer to "D. Colors" (page 36).

B. Categorizing

*Ask the students to look at the chart and categorize the men's wear by color: *red/white/blue*, for example, and by pattern; *solid/striped/checked*.

C. Practice with Word Order

**Have students practice word order with adjectives of color and pattern by asking each other questions about whether men should wear various color and pattern combinations.

S1: Should a man wear a red striped suit?

S2: Yes, he should./No, he shouldn't.

S2: Should a man wear green plaid slacks?

S1: Yes, he should./No, he shouldn't.

Students can refer to **Women's Wear** (page 36) and **Men's & Women's Wear** (page 37) for additional vocabulary.

D. Role Play

**Have students pretend they are in a men's clothing store. One student takes the role of the salesperson. The other takes the role of the customer (female students can pretend they are buying a gift for a male friend or relative). The salesperson asks the customer what he/she wants. The customer responds. The salesperson describes what is available and how much it costs. The customer discusses the item and decides whether or not to buy it.

Students can refer to **Numbers** (page 1) and **Money & Banking** (page 6) for additional vocabulary.

E. Discussion

*1. Have students ask each other what various men in the class are wearing.

S1: What's he wearing?

S2: Jeans, a red sport shirt, and a blue sweater.

S2: What's he wearing?

S1: <u>Gray slacks, a plaid shirt, and a green sport coat.</u>

**2. Have students talk about what type of men's clothing is appropriate in various situations in their countries.

> T: What do men wear to the office?
> What do men wear to school?
> What do men wear to a party?
> What do men wear to a restaurant?
> What do men wear to the movies?

WOMEN'S WEAR   Page 36

PRIMARY OBJECTIVE

Recognize and describe the women's clothing on the page.

CONVERSATIONAL OBJECTIVES

Talk about favorite colors, patterns, and clothes.
Discuss appropriate clothes for certain situations.
Discuss other students' appearance.

RELATED UNITS

Men's Wear (page 35), Men's & Women's Wear (page 37), Accessories (page 38)

CULTURAL COMMENTS

Women who work in offices usually wear a suit, a dress, or a skirt and blouse; a blouse and slacks is also appropiate in many offices.
The length of women's skirts changes often. Usually, the stylish length is just below the knees. But every few years, it becomes stylish to wear skirts above the knees. These short skirts are called mini-skirts. Sometimes it is stylish to wear skirts or dresses well below the knee, almost to the ankle.

VOCABULARY NOTES

Alternate Words

16—bra = brassiere

Usage

A handbag, clutch bag, and shoulder bag are all often referred to as a purse, bag, or pocketbook.

Panty hose cover the legs, hips, and waist. Stockings cover only the legs and do not go higher than the thighs. Tights are like panty hose, except that they are usually in bright colors and are made of a slightly thicker or heavier material.
*A formal dress worn to a party or other formal event is called a gown or evening gown.

RELATED IDIOMS AND EXPRESSIONS

tickled pink: very excited or pleased.
in black and white: proven or believed to be true because it is written on paper.
in the bag: unofficially achieved.

MINI-PRACTICE NOTES

Additional Structures

Introduce the structure from **Men's Wear** (page 35), and expand it by having students offer an alternative negative answer.

> Do you have a yellow suit?
> Yes, I do./No, I don't, but I have a pink suit.
> Do you have a flowered dress?
> Yes, I do./No, I don't, but I have a polka-dot dress.

FURTHER PRACTICE (Wall Chart Set 2)

A. Talk about Colors

*Have students ask each other about their favorite color.

> S1: What's your favorite color?
> S2: Purple.

Students can refer to "D. Colors" (page 35).

B. Talk about Patterns

*Have students ask each other about their favorite pattern.

> S1: What's your favorite pattern?
> S2: Polka dots.

Students can refer to "E. Patterns" (page 35).

C. Practice with Word Order

**Have students practice word order with adjectives of color and pattern by asking each other questions about whether women should wear various color and pattern combinations.

> S1: Should a woman wear a purple polka dot blouse?
> S2: Yes, she should./No, she shouldn't.
> S2: Should a woman wear yellow print slacks?
> S1: Yes, she should./No, she shouldn't.

Students can refer to **Men's Wear** (page 35) and **Men's & Women's Wear** (page 37) for additional vocabulary.

D. Role Play

**Have students pretend they are in a women's clothing store. One student takes the role of the salesperson. The other takes the role of the customer (male students can pretend they are buying a gift for a female friend or relative). The salesperson asks the customer what he/she wants. The customer responds. The salesperson describes what is available and how much it costs. The customer discusses the item and decides whether or not to buy it.

Students can refer to **Numbers** (page 1) and **Money & Banking** (page 6) for additional vocabulary.

E. Discussion

*1. Have students ask each other what various women in the class are wearing.

    S1: What's she wearing?

    S2: A flowered blouse and a turquoise skirt.

    S2: What's she wearing?

    S1: A black t-shirt and jeans.

**2. Have students talk about what type of women's clothing is appropriate in various situations in their countries.

    T: What do women wear to the office?
    What do women wear to the school?
    What do women wear to a party?
    What do women wear to a restaurant?
    What do women wear to the movies?

MEN'S & WOMEN'S WEAR   Page   37

PRIMARY OBJECTIVES

Recognize and describe the men's and women's clothing on the page.
Express the frequency with which students wear the clothes on the page, using *always*, *often*, *rarely*, and *never*.
Talk about the places on the body where clothes are worn.

CONVERSATIONAL OBJECTIVES

Talk about personal preferences in clothes.
Talk about what clothes indicate about the person who wears them.

RELATED UNITS

The Body (page 23), **Men's Wear** (page 35), **Women's Wear** (page 36), **Accessories** (page 38)

CULTURAL COMMENTS

Few people wear hats or caps in the United States. Men generally remove their hats when they go indoors. Women generally do not remove their hats indoors.

People generally wear gloves only when it is cold. Women sometimes wear thin white or black gloves on formal occasions.

VOCABULARY NOTES

Alternate Words

```
 1—coat = overcoat = topcoat (for men only)
16—shoelace = lace
22—robe = bathrobe
23—nightgown = nightie
```

Usage

Women's shoes like the ones in photo 13 are often called pumps. If the shoes have high heels, they are usually called heels or high heels. If the shoes have heels that are flat like men's heels, they are called flats.

Children often call pajamas pjs or jammies.

Wear is used as a noun to mean clothing, as in *men's wear*. It is also used as a verb to mean "to have on your body," as in "She wears a suit to work every day."

The singular of *men* is *man*. The singular of *women* is *woman*.

RELATED IDIOMS AND EXPRESSIONS

to take your hat off to someone or something: to salute; show respect or appreciation.
If I were in your shoes: If I were you.

MINI-PRACTICE NOTES

Additional Structure

*Have students talk about the appropriate time and place to wear the clothes on the page by introducing the following structure:

```
When do you wear a coat?
When I go outside.
When do you wear pajamas?
When I go to sleep.
When do you wear a sweater?
When it's cold.
```

Students may refer to **Weather & Seasons** (page 4) and **Action at Home** (page 26) for additional vocabulary.

FURTHER PRACTICE

A. Talk about Men's and Women's Wear

*Have students ask each other where to wear the clothing shown in the unit.

S1: Where do you wear <u>a hat</u>?

S2: <u>On my head</u>.

S2: Where do you wear <u>gloves</u>?

S1: <u>On my hands</u>.

Students may refer to **The Body** (pages 23 and 24) for additional vocabulary.

B. Practice with *Always, Often, Rarely, and Never*

**Have students name something they always wear, something they often wear, something they rarely wear, and something they never wear.

    S: I always wear <u>sandals in the summer</u>.
       I often wear <u>gloves when it's cold</u>.
       I rarely wear <u>a hat</u>.
       I never wear <u>sneakers to school</u>.

C. Discussion

**1. Ask students what they think clothes tell about people's personalities.

    T: What kind of person wears a bathrobe?
       What kind of person wears pajamas?
       What kind of person wears a hat?
       What kind of person wears a cap?
       What kind of person wears a cardigan sweater?
       What kind of person wears a crewneck sweater?
       What kind of person wears slippers?
       What kind of person wears sandals?

**2. Ask students to talk about their clothes.

    T: How much money do you spend on clothes?
       How many pairs of shoes do you have?
       Do you think you have many shoes or not enough? Why?
       Do you like to go shopping for clothes?
       What kind of clothes do you like to wear?

ACCESSORIES   Page 38

PRIMARY OBJECTIVES

Recognize and describe the accessories on the page.
Categorize accessories by the gender of people who use them.

CONVERSATIONAL OBJECTIVES

Talk about the kinds of jewelry students have and wear.
Express opinions about the kinds of jewelry men should and should not wear.

RELATED UNITS

The Body (page 23), Men's Wear (page 35), Women's Wear (page 36), Men's & Women's Wear (page 37)

CULTURAL COMMENTS

Many people think that men should not wear jewelry. However, some men wear rings, bracelets, earrings, and/or chains.

People who are married usually wear wedding rings, also called wedding bands, on the fourth finger of their left hand.

Photos 1–4 and 29–31 show men's and women's styles of the same item.

VOCABULARY NOTES

Alternate Words

    2—watch = wristwatch
    11—key ring = key chain
    12—stay = collar stay
    30—scarf = muffler
    31—handkerchief = hanky

Usage

Pearls are often referred to as a string of pearls.

A briefcase and an attaché case are similar, and the words are often used interchangeably.

A man's watch and the items in photos 10–16 are usually called men's accessories rather than jewelry.

A chain is often called a necklace when worn by a woman. A necklace often has a pendant or charm hanging from it. Chains worn by men are almost never called necklaces.

RELATED IDIOMS AND EXPRESSIONS

golden years or *golden age:* refers to ages over 65.
Every cloud has a silver lining: Every piece of bad news has some good or redeeming news.

MINI-PRACTICE NOTES

Additional Structure

Introduce the structure from Men's & Women's Wear (page 37) to practice always, often, rarely, and never.

    Do you ever wear a watch?
    Yes, I always wear one.
    Do you ever wear cuff links?
    No, I never wear them.

FURTHER PRACTICE

A. Talk about Accessories

*1. Have students ask each other what kind of accessories they have. They should be able to combine gems and metals in their questions.

> S1: Do you have ruby earrings?
> S2: Yes, I do./No, I don't.
> S2: Do you have gold cuff links?
> S1: Yes, I do./No, I don't.

*2. Have students talk about where people wear accessories.

> S1: What do people wear on their ears?
> S2: They wear earrings.
> S2: What do people wear on their wrist?
> S1: They wear a watch or a bracelet.

Students may refer to **The Body** (pages 23 and 24) for additional vocabulary.

B. Categorizing

*Have students work together to put accessories into categories.

1. Accessories used only by men
2. Accessories used only by women
3. Accessories used by both men and women

C. Discussion.

**Ask students to talk about the kinds of jewelry they like to wear.

> T: Do you like to wear jewelry?
> What kind of jewelry do you usually wear?
> When do you wear jewelry?
> What's your favorite gem?
> Which do you like better, gold or silver?
> Do you think men should wear jewelry?
> What kinds of jewelry do you think men should and shouldn't wear?
> Do you think women should wear jewelry?
> What kinds of jewelry do you think women should and shouldn't wear?
> Do people wear different kinds of jewelry in your country?

PRIMARY OBJECTIVE

Recognize and describe the types of houses on the page.

CONVERSATIONAL OBJECTIVES

Talk about types of housing that students have lived in.
Express opinions about a dream house.

RELATED UNITS

The Backyard and Garden (page 40), **The Living Room** (page 41), **The Dining Room** (page 42), **The Bedroom** (page 43), **The Bathroom** (page 44), **The Kitchen** (page 45), **The Nursery** (page 47)

CULTURAL COMMENTS

The apartment buildings in suburbs and small towns are usually smaller than those in cities. Houses of all types are found in most suburbs and small towns.
A floor plan usually lists the dimensions of each room so people can know how big a house or apartment is.

VOCABULARY NOTES

Usage

Each individual dwelling within an apartment building is called an apartment, or occasionally a (rental) unit.
In some parts of the United States, a duplex is not a two-family house, but rather an apartment that takes up parts of two floors of an apartment building and has a stairway within the apartment. Most apartments take up part of only one floor of an apartment building.
A house is a home when it has furniture and people in it.

Additional Words

housework: jobs like cooking, cleaning, and doing laundry.
housewife, or househusband: a woman or man who stays home and does housework instead of working at a job outside the house.

RELATED IDIOMS AND EXPRESSIONS

Home Sweet Home: I'm happy that I'm home.
lived-in: comfortable.

MINI-PRACTICE NOTES

Additional Structure

Continue the mini-practice structure, using the present tense instead of the present perfect.

> Do you live in <u>an apartment building</u>?
> Yes, I do./No, I don't.

FURTHER PRACTICE (Wall Charts set 2)

A. Talk about Housing

*Have students ask each other about the kind of housing they live in.

> S1: What kind of house do you live in?
> S2: I live in <u>an apartment building</u>.
> S2: What kind of house do you live in?
> S1: I live in a <u>two-family house</u>.

B. Role Play

**Have students work in pairs. One student takes the role of a real estate agent. The other student takes the role of a person who wants to rent or buy a house or an apartment. The real estate agent asks the customer what he/she is looking for. The customer responds. The agent tries to sell or rent what he/she has available.

C. Discussion

**1. Ask students to talk about their dream house: the kind of house they would like to have if they could have any house they wanted. Ask them to describe the kind of house it would be, how many bedrooms and bathrooms it would have, and what it would look like from the outside.

Students can refer to **The Backyard & Garden** (page 40), **The Living Room** (page 41), **The Dining Room** (page 42), **The Bedroom** (page 43), **The Bathroom** (page 44), and **The Kitchen** (page 45) for additional vocabulary.

**2. Ask students to describe the housing situation in their countries.

> T: Do most people buy houses or rent them?
> Do most people buy apartments or rent them?
> Do most people who live in the city live in houses or apartments?
> Do older people live alone, or do they live with their married children?
> Do most single people live in houses or in apartments?

**3. Have some students describe the floor plan of their house or apartment. Other students at the board can draw the floor plan as it is being described.

THE BACKYARD AND GARDEN

PRIMARY OBJECTIVES

Recognize and describe the backyard and garden items on the page.
Express preferences among flowers.

CONVERSATIONAL OBJECTIVES

Talk about things students have or would like to have in their backyards.
Discuss planting a vegetable garden.

RELATED UNITS

Weather & Seasons (page 4), **Fruit** (page 15), **Vegetables** (page 16), **Housing** (page 39), **Land & Water** (page 54), **Hobbies & Games** (page 79)

CULTURAL COMMENTS

Americans spend a lot of time in their backyards and gardens. On weekend nights, weather permitting, many American families cook hotdogs, hamburgers, steaks, or chicken on the barbecue. This is called cooking out, or having a cookout.

People often send or bring flowers from a florist (flower shop) or from their own backyards on several different occasions: when invited to dinner, when someone is sick, on Mother's Day, when celebrating somebody's birthday or wedding anniversary, or simply as a gesture of friendship.

VOCABULARY NOTES

Alternate Words

```
 5—lounge chair = chaise lounge
 7—barbecue = grill
12—bush = shrub
```

Additional Words

weed: a wild plant that grows in your garden that you do not want to grow there.
to weed: to remove weeds.

RELATED IDIOMS AND EXPRESSIONS

to grow like a weed: to grow very quickly.
The grass is always greener on the other side of the fence: You usually want the things you don't or can't have, but once you have them, you don't want them so much anymore.

to stop and smell the roses: to take a moment to enjoy the simple pleasures of life.
fresh as a daisy: very fresh or refreshed.

MINI-PRACTICE NOTES

Alternate Structure

Introduce the following alternate response:

> Do you like <u>roses</u>?
>
> Yes. But I prefer <u>tulips</u>./No. I prefer <u>tulips</u>.

Additional Structures

Introduce the following structure:

Have you ever seen <u>a daisy</u>?
Yes, I have./No, I haven't.

Introduce the following structure:

Do you have <u>azaleas</u> in your country?
Yes, we do./No, we don't.

FURTHER PRACTICE

A. Talk about the Backyard and Garden

*Have students ask each other about the things they have in their backyards and gardens.

> S1: Do you have <u>a patio</u> in your backyard?
>
> S2: Yes, I do./No, I don't, but I have a vegetable garden.
>
> S2: Do you have <u>daisies</u> in your garden?
>
> S1: Yes, I do./No, I don't, but I have <u>tulips and daffodils</u>.

B. Discussion

**1. Ask students to talk about their backyards.

> T: Do you have a backyard?
> Do you have a garden?
> What do you like to do in your backyard or garden?/What would you do if you had a backyard or garden?
> Do you like to work in your backyard and garden?
> Do you like to mow the lawn?
> Do you like to barbecue in your backyard?

**2. Ask students to talk about flowers.

> T: Which is your favorite flower?
> Do people give each other flowers on special occasions in your country? If so, when?

C. Activity: Planting a Vegetable Garden

**Have students work in small groups to create a set of instructions for how to plant a vegetable garden. They should tell when to plant, when to rake, when to water the garden, and when to pick the vegetables.

PRIMARY OBJECTIVES

Recognize and describe the living room furniture on the page.
Recognize and describe the location of the furniture on the page using *in front of, behind,*
and *on.*

CONVERSATIONAL OBJECTIVES

Talk about the furniture in students' living rooms.
Discuss buying living room furniture.

RELATED UNITS

Housing (page 39), **The Dining Room** (page 42), **The Bedroom** (page 43), **The Bathroom** (page
44), **The Kitchen** (page 45)

CULTURAL COMMENTS

A fireplace is generally found in the living room, although other houses have fireplaces in
other rooms as well. Apartments rarely have fireplaces.
The living room in the photo has a lot of furniture. Living rooms generally do not have so
much furniture.
The living room is the place where most people entertain friends, neighbors, and guests.
Many people have a television and a stereo system (see **Electronics**, page 51) in their living
room. Other people keep these devices in a room called the family room or the den, a
room which is used for more informal or family entertaining.

VOCABULARY NOTES

Alternate Words

> 4—club chair = armchair
> 10—wall unit = cabinet = hutch
> 25—ottoman = footrest = hassock

Usage

A rug covers part of the floor; a carpet covers the whole floor. However, people often use
the two interchangeably. A carpet is often called wall-to-wall carpeting because it covers
the floor from one wall to the other.
A drape is usually made of heavy material and is often tied back, as in photo 14. Generally, a curtain is made of light or thin material and completely covers the window.
Some people have both curtains and drapes in their living room.
Drapes usually come in pairs, or sets, and are usually referred to in the plural: Pull back
the drapes.

FURTHER PRACTICE (Wall Chart Set 1)

A. Talk about the Living Room

*1. Have the students ask each other what's in their living rooms.

> S1: Do you have <u>a club chair</u> in your living room?
>
> S2: No, I don't.
>
> S2: Do you have <u>a couch</u> in your living room?
>
> S1: Yes, I do.

**2. Have some students describe all the furniture in their living room and explain where the furniture is located. Other students at the board draw the room with the furniture as it is being described.

B. Role Play

**Have students pretend they are in a furniture store buying living room furniture. Students work in pairs. One student takes the role of the salesperson. The other takes the role of the customer. The salesperson asks the customer what he/she wants. The customer responds. The salesperson describes what is available and how much it costs. The customer discusses the item and decides whether or not to buy it.

> SALESPERSON: May I help you?
>
> CUSTOMER: Yes, I'm looking for a <u>coffee table</u>.
>
> SALESPERSON: <u>We have this one. It's on sale for $250.00</u>.
>
> CUSTOMER: It's very nice. I'll buy it.

Students can refer to **Numbers** (page 1) and **Money & Banking** (page 6) for vocabulary.

THE DINING ROOM   Page   42

PRIMARY OBJECTIVES

Recognize and describe the dining room items on the page.
Recognize and describe the locations of the items on the page.

CONVERSATIONAL OBJECTIVES

Talk about students' dining rooms.
Discuss various ways to set a table.
Discuss inviting someone for dinner.

RELATED UNITS

Housing (page 39), **The Living Room** (page 41), **The Bedroom** (page 43), **The Bathroom** (page 44), **The Kitchen** (page 45)

CULTURAL COMMENTS

Some families have an eating table in both the kitchen and the dining room. They generally eat most of their meals in the kitchen, and use the dining room for special or formal occasions or for entertaining friends.

The head and foot of the table (the seats at the narrow ends of the table) are usually places of respect, saved for the most important people at the table. During family dinners, the mother and father usually sit at the head and the foot of the table.

People generally do not use separate salad forks and dinner forks except in formal occasions.

VOCABULARY NOTES

Usage

The side armrests of armchairs are called arms. Armchairs are usually placed at the head and foot of the table.

The plural of *knife* is *knives*.

Additional Words

silverware: collective word for knives, forks, and spoons.
place setting: the silverware, china, and glasses that are usually set on a table at a person's place.
crystal: fine water and wine glasses.
dishes: see **The Kitchen** (page 45).
china: see **The Kitchen** (page 45).

RELATED IDIOMS AND EXPRESSIONS

to set the table: to place the plates and silverware on the table.
to clear the table: to remove the plates and silverware from the table.
to do the dishes: to wash the dishes.
to have company: to have guests come to your house.

FURTHER PRACTICE (Wall Chart Set 2)

A. Talk about the Dining Room

*Have students ask each other about the dining room on the chart.

>   S1: Do you like this dining room?
>   S2: Yes, I do./No, I don't.
>   S1: Would you like to have a dining room like this one?
>   S2: Yes, I would./No, I wouldn't.

B. Role Play

**Have students role play inviting someone to dinner. One student offers the invitation and tells the other student the day, time, and place. The other student accepts or declines. You may want to introduce appropriate phrases for offering and declining invitations, such as:

Would you like to come to dinner?
I'd like you to come to dinner.
Thanks very much, I'd like to.
I'm sorry, I can't.

C. Discussion

*1. Point to the photo and ask students to describe the dining room.

> T: What furniture is in the photo?
> How many people are coming to dinner?
> What's on the table?
> What's on the server?
> What color is the door?
> What color are the seats?

**2. Have some students describe how to set a table. They can use the order of the place settings on the table on the chart, or they can describe how they set their own table. Students should mention the placement of the fork(s), spoon(s), knife, plate(s), and glass(es). Other students at the board can draw pictures of the table as it is being described. If the placement is different from the one shown on the chart, ask students to say how it's different.

**3. Have students discuss their opinions of the type of dining room on the chart.

> T: Do you know people who have a dining room like the one on the chart?
> What kind of people probably live in this house?
> What kind of food do people eat in a dining room like this one?
> Would you feel comfortable eating in this room?

THE BEDROOM   Page   43

PRIMARY OBJECTIVES

Recognize and describe the bedding and furniture on the page.

CONVERSATIONAL OBJECTIVES

Describe students' own bedroom.
Describe what students do in their bedroom.
Discuss buying bedding and bedroom furniture.

RELATED UNITS

Action at Home (page 26), Housing (page 39)

CULTURAL COMMENTS

The bedroom on this page is considered large and well-furnished. It is more likely to be found in a house than in an apartment.
Beds and bedding come in different sizes. The sizes, from largest to smallest, are as

follows: king-size, queen-size, double/full-size, and twin-size. Double and twin-size beds are generally for one person. Double, queen, and king-size beds are generally for two people. The bed in the photo is a double bed.

Many Americans keep a television in their bedroom. They often watch television in bed before going to sleep or in the morning while getting dressed.

VOCABULARY NOTES

Alternate Words

9—chest (of drawers) = bureau

Usage

Dresser and *chest of drawers* are often used interchangeably.

Additional Words

bedtime: the hour when people go to sleep.
bed and board, or room and board: somewhere to sleep and have meals.
bed and breakfast: a small hotel, inn, or house that rents rooms and provides breakfast for its guests.

RELATED IDIOMS AND EXPRESSIONS

bedtime: the hour when people go to sleep.
bed and board, or room and board: somewhere to sleep and have meals.
bed and breakfast: a small hotel, inn, or house that rents rooms and provides breakfast for its guests.

MINI-PRACTICE NOTES

Usage

On may be used instead of *on top of* in the students' responses. Similarly, *under* may be used instead of *underneath*.

FURTHER PRACTICE

A. Talk about the Bedroom

*Have students ask each other about their own bedroom and the one in the picture.

    S1: Do you like this bedroom?
    S2: Yes, I do./No, I don't.
    S1: Is your bedroom like this one?
    S2: Yes, it is./No, it isn't.

B. Discussion

**Ask students about their bedrooms and what they do in their bedroom.

    T: Do you spend a lot of time in your bedroom?
    Do you make your bed every morning?

Is your bedroom neat or messy?
Do you like to read and watch television in bed?

C. Role Play: Buying Bedding

**Bedding is another word for sheets, pillows, pillowcases, and blankets. You can usually
buy all these things in the same store. Beds come in four sizes in the United States:
single (for one person), double (for one or two people), queen-size (a little bigger than
double), and king-size (a little bigger than queen-size).
Have students take turns playing the customer and the salesclerk at a bedding store. The
customer asks to buy sheets and pillowcases. The clerk asks what size bed the customer
has and what color sheets the customer wants.

THE BATHROOM   Page   44

PRIMARY OBJECTIVES

Recognize and describe the bathroom articles and appliances on the page.
Recognize and describe the location of the items on the page.

CONVERSATIONAL OBJECTIVES

Describe students' morning bathroom routine.
Talk about similarities and differences between public bathrooms and the bathrooms at
    home.
Talk about hygiene in the U.S. and in other countries.

RELATED UNITS

Cosmetics & Toiletries (page 25), Action at Home (page 26)

CULTURAL COMMENTS

Many bathrooms, especially bathrooms in city apartments, have a shower without a
    bathtub underneath; this is called a stall shower. Some bathrooms have a stall shower
    and a separate bathtub.
Americans are often embarrassed when they talk about the bathroom and do not usually
    talk about the bathroom in public.
The bathroom in restaurants and other public places is usually called the rest room, the
men's or ladies' room, or the lavatory.

VOCABULARY NOTES

Alternate Words

15—medicine cabinet = medicine chest
16—cup = tumbler

Additional Words

Toilet seat: the part of the toilet where you sit.
lid: the top of the toilet that closes over the toilet and toilet seat.
spigot: the part of the sink or bathtub where the water comes out.

RELATED IDIOMS AND EXPRESSIONS

bathroom humor: remarks or jokes that are considered very vulgar.

MINI-PRACTICE NOTES

Additional Structure

Introduce the plural.

> Where are the <u>towels</u>?
> They're <u>on the sink</u>.
> Where are the <u>toothbrushes</u>?
> They're <u>in the toothbrush holder</u>.

FURTHER PRACTICE

A. Practice with *Above* and *Below*

Have students ask each other questions to practice their understanding of *above* and *below*.

> S1: What's above the <u>towel rack</u>?
> S2: The <u>light switch</u>.
> S2: What's below the <u>shower head</u>?
> S1: The <u>hot water faucet and the cold water faucet</u>.

B. Discussion

**1. Ask students about bathroom habits in their country.

> T: Do people usually take showers or baths in your country?
> Which do you like better—a shower or a bath?
> Do you use hot water or cold water?
> Do you usually take a shower/bath in the morning or at night?

**2. Ask students to describe their bathroom routine. Example:
First I wash my face. Then I brush my teeth. Then I take a shower and wash my hair.
  Then I dry off. Then I put on deodorant. Then I comb my hair.
Students may refer to **Cosmetics & Toiletries** (page 25) and **Action at Home** (page 26) for
  additional vocabulary.

C. Activity: Similarities and Differences

Write the words *Similarities* and *Differences* in two columns on the board and explain their
  meanings. Then ask students to name some similarities between the bathroom in their
  home and the bathroom in a public building. Then ask them to name some differences.
Example:

Similarities	Differences
1. Both have sinks.	1. No toothbrushes in public bathroom.
2. Both have toilets.	2. No medicine cabinet in public bathroom.
3. Both have soap.	3. No paper towels in the bathroom in my house.
4. Both have mirrors.	4. No bathtub or shower in public bathroom.

THE KITCHEN Page 45

PRIMARY OBJECTIVES

Recognize and describe the appliances and other kitchen items on the page.
Recognize and describe the location of appliances and kitchen items on the page.

CONVERSATIONAL OBJECTIVES

Express opinions about the kitchen on the page.
Describe students' own kitchens.
Describe what they do in their kitchen.

RELATED UNIT

Kitchenware (page 46)

CULTURAL COMMENTS

The kitchen is generally a gathering place for family discussions as well as for informal
   entertaining of close friends and neighbors. Important family decisions are often made
   sitting around the kitchen table.
The kitchen on this page is considered very large, modern, and well-equipped. It is probably an "eat-in" kitchen, although the table and chairs are not shown. Such a kitchen is
   more likely to be found in a house in a suburb or small town than in a city apartment.

VOCABULARY NOTES

Alternate Words

    11—refrigerator = fridge = ice box
    30—aluminum foil = tin foil

Usage

Saran wrap is a brand name now used generically for all items of its type.

Additional Words

dishes: refers generally to plates, cups, and saucers.
china: dishes made of fine porcelain.

RELATED IDIOMS AND EXPRESSIONS

to cook one's own goose: to ruin one's own opportunity.

MINI-PRACTICE NOTES

Additional Structures

Students are asked to describe the location of one item or object in terms of another,
   using *on* and *next to*.
Continue the exercise, introducing *in front of*, *behind*, *to the right of*, and *to the left of*.

   Where's the refrigerator?
   It's to the right of the dishwasher.

Introduce the plural.

   Where are the bowls?
   They're on the counter.

FURTHER PRACTICE (Wall Chart Set 1)

A. Talk about the Kitchen

*Have students describe the items in the kitchen.

   T: What's on the counter next to the stove?
   What's on the tray?
   What's on the stove?
   What's on the counter next to the sink?
   What's on the cake stand?

**2. Have some students describe their own kitchen. Other students at the board draw
   pictures of the kitchen as it is being described. Be sure each student mentions the
   basic kitchen appliances (sink, refrigerator, stove) and tells where these items are in
   the room.
Students can refer to **Kitchenware** (page 46) for additional vocabulary.

B. Discussion

**Ask students what they do in their kitchens.

   T: Do you eat in the kitchen? Which meals do you eat in the kitchen?
   How many hours a day do you spend in the kitchen?
   Do you invite guests or friends into your kitchen?
   Who does the cooking in your house?
   Do you think men should do the cooking?
   Do you think women should do the cooking?

PRIMARY OBJECTIVES

Recognize and describe the kitchenware and utensils on the page.
Understand the purpose and uses of the kitchenware and utensils on the page.

CONVERSATIONAL OBJECTIVES

Talk about different methods of cooking and the appliances used in each method.
Recognize, describe, and use verbs associated with cooking.
Make up and explain recipes.

RELATED UNIT

The Kitchen (page 45)

CULTURAL COMMENTS

Almost every American kitchen has a frying pan, a pot, a knife, a spatula, a ladle, a
coffeemaker or coffee pot, and a toaster.

VOCABULARY NOTES

Usage

A casserole is sometimes called a casserole pot to avoid confusion with the food inside of
it, which is also called a casserole.
The kitchenware on the page can be classified under three general categories.
Pots and pans/cookware: general terms used for cooking items (items 1, 3–5, 7–10).
Appliances: generally electronic kitchenware items used for cooking or preparing food (items
14–21).
Utensils: generally hand-held tools used to help cook or prepare food (items 11–13, 22–31).

Alternate Words

1—double boiler = Dutch oven
2—lid = cover = top
7—roaster = roasting pan
28—whisk = wire whisk
30—peeler = vegetable peeler = potato peeler

RELATED IDIOMS AND EXPRESSIONS

out of the frying pan and into the fire: refers to a situation that goes from bad to worse.
to fly off the handle: to become uncontrollably angry.

MINI-PRACTICE NOTES

Alternate Structure

Introduce a different way of asking the purposes of kitchenware items.

> What do you use a toaster for?
> To make toast.
> What do you use a coffeemaker for?
> To make coffee.

FURTHER PRACTICE (Wall Chart Set 1)

A. Talk about Kitchenware

*1. Have students ask each other if they have ever used the objects on the chart.

> S1: Have you ever used a toaster?
> S2: Yes, I have.
> S2: Have you ever used a microwave oven?
> S1: No, I haven't.

**2. Ask students what foods they cook in the various pots and pans in items 1–7.

> T: What do you cook in a roaster?
> What do you cook in a frying pan?
> What do you cook in a pot?

B. Categorizing

*Have students categorize objects by use.

> T: You are going to bake a cake. List all the objects you might use to bake a cake.
> S1: A beater or a mixer.
> S2: A spatula.
> T: You are going to make eggs. Name all the objects you might use to make eggs.
> S1: A frying pan.
> S2: A grater (for a cheese omelet).

C. Discussion

**Talk about the verbs associated with some of the nouns on the chart.

double boiler—*boil*	mixer—*mix*
frying pan—*fry*	beater—*beat*
roaster—*roast*	strainer—*strain*
rolling pin—*roll*	grater—*grate*
measuring cup—*measure*	peeler—*peel*
blender—*blend*	whisk—*whisk*

Dictate a recipe using some of the verbs above. Have students volunteer to dictate a recipe while other students write it on the board.

Students can refer to **The Supermarket** (page 13 and 14), **Fruit** (page 15), **Vegetables** (page 16), **The Menu** (page 17), and **Fast Foods & Snacks** (page 18) for vocabulary.

THE NURSERY

PRIMARY OBJECTIVES

Recognize and describe the items on the page.
Use the prepositions *in* and *on* with the items on the page.

CONVERSATIONAL OBJECTIVES

Talk about things babies and children do at different ages.
Describe students' feelings about babies.
Talk about students' knowledge of how to take care of a baby.

RELATED UNITS

Action at Home (page 26), **The Bedroom** (page 43)

CULTURAL COMMENTS

A nursery is a bedroom for a baby.
People who live in big houses turn an entire room into a nursery when they have a baby. People who do not have enough space for a separate nursery keep a crib and a play-pen in their bedroom or living room.
There are two kinds of diapers: disposable and cloth. Disposable diapers are made from paper and plastic and are thrown out after a few hours. Cloth diapers are made from cotton or polyester and must be washed after each wearing.
A baby's age is given in months until he or she is about two years old. Then it is given in years. We generally say "eighteen months old" rather than "one and a half years old," and "three years old" rather than "thirty-six months old."

VOCABULARY NOTES

Alternate Words

12—baby = infant

RELATED IDIOMS AND EXPRESSIONS

baby-face: a very young-looking face.
to be a baby: to act young or immature.

FURTHER PRACTICE

A. Practice with Prepositions

*Have students ask each other questions to practice *in* and *on*.

S1: Where should I put the baby?

S2: Put the baby in the carriage.

S2: Where should I put the baby?

S1: Put the baby on the rug.

B. Discussion

**Ask students about who takes care of babies in their country.

> T: Do men ever take care of babies?
> Who feeds the baby?
> Who changes the baby's diapers?
> Who puts the baby to sleep?

C. Activity:

**Have students work in groups to prepare a schedule for taking care of a baby. Each schedule should tell when to change the baby's diapers, when to give the baby milk, and when to put the baby to sleep.
Example:

7:00 A.M.	Baby wakes up
7:15 A.M.	Change diaper
7:30 A.M.	Give first bottle
9:00 A.M.	Take baby for walk in stroller
9:30 A.M.	Change diaper
12:30 P.M.	Give second bottle of milk
1:00 P.M.	Baby takes afternoon nap
3:00 P.M.	Change diapers

D. Role Play

**Have students take turns playing a parent and a baby-sitter. (A baby-sitter takes care of a baby while his or her parents are out of the house.) The baby-sitter asks where the milk, bottles, bibs, and diapers are. The baby-sitter also asks if the parent has any special instructions about feeding the baby or when to put him or her to bed. The parent gives the baby-sitter all the necessary information.

THE PLAYGROUND   Page   48

PRIMARY OBJECTIVES

Recognize and describe the objects in the playground.
Recognize and describe the locations of the people in the playground.
Recognize and describe the actions being performed by the people in the playground.

CONVERSATIONAL OBJECTIVES

Talk about typical activities at a playground.
Talk about personal experiences at a playground.

RELATED UNITS

Action at the Gym (page 27), Action at School (page 28), The Nursery (page 47)

CULTURAL COMMENTS

A playground is a small park intended just for children. It is usually found in big cities where there is not enough room for a park. There is generally no grass in a playground, only cement or asphalt on the ground. Most playgrounds have sandboxes, jungle gyms, swings, see-saws, and slides for small children.

Young children and babies are usually taken to a playground or park by an adult. The adult supervises the children at play. When children reach the age of five or six years old, they generally go to the playground or park with other children rather than with adults.

VOCABULARY NOTES

Alternate Words

    7—jungle gym = monkey bars
    10—pail = bucket
    13—sneakers = tennis shoes = gym shoes
    4—tricycle = trike

RELATED IDIOMS AND EXPRESSIONS

Go *fly a kite*: Stop bothering me. Go away.

a see-saw *battle*: a fight, battle, or game in which the advantage switches constantly from one side to the other.

MINI-PRACTICE NOTES

Introduce the plural.

    Where are they?
    They're in the sandbox.

FURTHER PRACTICE

A. Talk about the Playground

*Have students point to a person in the picture and ask each other what that person is doing.

    S1: What's she doing (1)?
    S2: She's sitting on the see-saw.
    S2: What's he doing (4)?
    S1: He's riding a tricycle.

B. Discussion

**1. Ask students about playgrounds.

T: Do/Did you take your children or younger brothers and sister to the playground?
How old were you when you stopped going to playgrounds?
Do parents take children to playgrounds in your country?
How are playgrounds in your country the same as and different from the playground in the photos?

**2. Have students take turns describing what is happening in each of the pictures on the page. For example, in the top left picture: two girls are sitting on one see-saw and a mother and her child are at the other see-saw.

THE LAUNDRY ROOM   Page   49

PRIMARY OBJECTIVES

Recognize and describe the objects on the page.
Recognize and describe the locations of the objects on the page.

CONVERSATIONAL OBJECTIVES

Talk about the uses for the objects on the page.
Talk about the kinds of housework students have done.
Talk about electricity in the U.S. and in their country.

RELATED UNIT

Action at Home (page 26)

CULTURAL COMMENTS

People who live in apartments do not usually have laundry rooms. They usually have a closet, called a broom closet, where they keep a broom, a mop, an iron, a vacuum cleaner, a dustpan, and an ironing board. They usually do not have a washer and dryer in their apartment. Instead, they go to a store called a laundromat, where they pay to use laundry machines; or they may pay to use a washer and dryer in a public area of their apartment building.
Many people take their fine clothes, like wool sweaters, coats, and jackets, suits, ties, and silk dresses and blouses, to the dry cleaners because they cannot wash these items at home or in a laundromat.

VOCABULARY NOTES
Alternate Words

9—vacuum cleaner = vacuum

RELATED IDIOMS AND EXPRESSIONS

to take someone to the cleaners: to charge someone too much.
to iron out: to remove or find an answer to (a problem or difficulty).

MINI-PRACTICE NOTES

Additional Structures

Continue the mini-practice, introducing *above* and *below*.
The iron is *above* the ironing board.
The bucket is *below* the mop.

FURTHER PRACTICE (Wall Chart Set 2)

A. Talk about the Laundry Room

*1. Have students ask each other about the laundry room objects in the closet (items 1–14).

  S1: Have you ever used a <u>whisk broom</u>?

  S2: Yes, I have./No I haven't.

  S2: Have you ever used a <u>carpet sweeper</u>?

  S1: Yes, I have./No, I haven't.

**2. Have students ask each other about the function of the laundry room objects in the closet (items 1–14).

  S1: What do you do with <u>an iron</u>?

  S2: <u>Iron clothes.</u>

  S2: What do you do with a <u>vacuum cleaner</u>?

  S1: <u>Clean rugs or carpets.</u>

B. Discussion

**1. Ask students about their laundry.

  T: Do you do your own laundry? If not, who does it?
  Do you think a man should do his own laundry?
  Do you have a washing machine?
  Do you have a dryer?
  Do you wash some of your clothes by hand?
  Do you use a dryer, or do you dry your clothes on a clothesline?
  Do you like to do laundry?
  Do you like to iron?

**2. Ask students about electricity in their countries.

  T: Do all houses in your country have electricity?
  Do you use 110 or 220 volts?
  How many outlets are there in most rooms?
  How many prongs do your plugs have?
  Do you leave a light on when you leave the house at night?
  Do you ever use an extension cord? What do you use it for?

PRIMARY OBJECTIVES

Recognize and describe the tools on the page.
Recognize and talk about uses for the tools on the page.

CONVERSATIONAL OBJECTIVES

Talk about personal experience with tools.
Express opinions about working with tools.
Express opinions about the kind of people who like to use tools and work with their hands.

RELATED UNITS

Housing (page 39), **The Backyard and Garden** (page 40), **Construction** (page 53)

CULTURAL COMMENTS

Many people keep all their tools in a room in their basement called a workshop or tool-
room. People who have a workshop in their houses like to work with tools and often
build things in the workshop. Some people keep their tools in their garage.
Working with tools is often called handiwork. It was usually thought of as men's work in
the U.S., but recently many women have begun to use tools and do handiwork.
People who do not know how to use tools often hire a person called a handyman to do
their handiwork for them.
In apartment buildings, the person who fixes things for people in the building is either the
handyman or the superintendent, who is often called "the super" for short.

RELATED IDIOMS AND EXPRESSIONS

fix-it or Mr./Ms. Fix-it: someone skilled at using tools and fixing things; a handyman.
odd jobs: occasional or miscellaneous jobs. Usually refers to work done by a handyman or
a Mr. Fix-it.
to bury the hatchet (SYN to let bygones be bygones): to settle an argument or dispute and
become friendly.

MINI-PRACTICE NOTES

Additional Structure

Continue the mini-practice, having students ask each other which tools are used together.

Do you use a <u>hammer</u> with a <u>chisel</u>?
Yes, you do.
Do you use a screwdriver with a paint pan?
No, you don't. You use <u>a paintbrush</u> with <u>a paint pan</u>.

FURTHER PRACTICE (Wall Chart Set 2)

A. Talk about Tools

*Have students ask each other what various tools are used for.

> S1: What do you use a <u>roller</u> for?
>
> S2: For <u>painting walls</u>.
>
> S2: What do you use a <u>saw</u> far?
>
> S1: For <u>cutting wood</u>.

B. Activity: Taking A Poll

**Make three columns on the board and label them *Agree*, *Disagree*, and *Not sure*. Then ask the students their opinions about these statements. Have students answer with *Yes, I agree*, *No, I disagree*, or *I'm not sure* and put a check in the appropriate column. Have one student tally the results on the board. Then ask students to discuss the reasons for their opinions.

> T: Men can fix things better than women.
> Some people have a special talent for fixing things.
> Older people can fix things better than younger people.
> Working with tools is dangerous.
> Working with tools is boring.
> Working with tools is creative.

C. Discussion

**1. Ask students to name various household jobs that they would like to do. Have them tell which tools they would need.

> T: What would you like to do?
>
> S: I'd like to <u>hang a picture</u>.
>
> T: What tools do you need?
>
> S: A <u>nail</u> and a <u>hammer</u>.

**2. Ask students how they feel about working with tools.

> T: Are you good with your hands?
> Do you like to work with tools? Why/Why not?
> If you could work with tools, what would you rather do—build something or fix something? Why?

ELECTRONICS

Page 51

PRIMARY OBJECTIVES

Recognize and describe the electronic objects on the page.
Express preferences about the electronic items on the page.

CONVERSATIONAL OBJECTIVES

Express opinions about electronics.
Talk about personal experience with electronics.
Record an answering machine message.

RELATED UNITS

The Office (page 20), **The Living Room** (page 41), **The Bedroom** (page 43)

CULTURAL COMMENTS

Most electronic items are extremely expensive when they are first sold in the United States.
But gradually, their price comes down and almost every American can afford to buy
them. The first calculators in the U.S. cost more than $100. Now you can buy one for
less than $10, and most people have one. VCRs were once very expensive as well, but
now more than half the families in the United States have one.
Some people do not like talking to an answering machine and will not leave a message if
a machine answers the phone.
Walkman is a brand name of personal cassette player. But like Jello (gelatin) and Band-
Aid (bandages), the brand name is now used generically for all items of its type.

VOCABULARY NOTES

Alternate Words

    6—stereo system = stereo
    22—telephone = phone

Usage

Headphone is often referred to in the plural: *headphones*.
A video cassette is often referred to as a videotape.
An amplifier is often called an amp.

Additional Words

receiver: a combination of an amplifier and tuner.
portable stereo cassette player/box/boom box: a portable radio and cassette player. It is
usually much larger than the cassette player in photo 17.

RELATED IDIOMS AND EXPRESSIONS

Hold the phone: Wait a minute.
to call up: to call someone on the phone.

MINI-PRACTICE NOTES

Alternate Structure

Introduce the following structure:

> Which electronic item would you like to have?
> I'd like to have *an answering machine.*

FURTHER PRACTICE (Wall Chart Set 2)

A. Talk about Electronics

*Have students ask each other if they have the electronic objects on the chart.

> S1: Do you have a television?
> S2: Yes, I do./No, I don't.
> S2: Do you have a clock radio?
> S1: Yes, I do./No, I don't.

B. Role Play

**Students work in pairs. One student writes an original message for his/her answering machine and reads it aloud. The other student listens to the message and leaves his/her own message. If you have access to a tape recorder, you may want to record the students' messages.

C. Discussion

**1. Ask students how they feel about answering machines.

> T: Do you have an answering machine? Why/why not?
> Do any of your friends have answering machines?
> Do you like leaving messages on other people's answering machines? Why/why not?
> Do you ever hang up without leaving a message on an answering machine?

**2. Ask students about their preferences in electronic equipment.

> T: Which do you like better—compact disc players or tape decks? Why?
> Which do you like better—tape decks or cassette players? Why?
> Which do you like better—compact discs or records? Why?
> Which do you like better—radios or tape recorders? Why?
> Which do you like better—Walkmen or cassette players? Why?
> Which do you like better—turntables or tape decks? Why?

**3. Ask students to name related electronic objects.

> T: If you buy a turntable, what else do you need?
> S: An amplifier, a tuner, a speaker/speakers, and records.

FURTHER PRACTICE (Wall Chart Set 2)

A. Talk about Electronics

*1. Have students ask each other if they have the electornic objects on the chart.

> S1: Do you have a typewriter?
> S2: Yes, I do./No, I don't.

**2. Have students ask and answer questions about their own experiences with the electronic equipment on the chart.

> S1: Have you ever used a computer?
> S2: Yes, I have.
> S1: Did you like it?
> S2: Yes, I did./No, I didn't.
> S2: Have you ever used a video camera?
> S1: No, I haven't.
> S2: Would you like to use one?
> S1: Yes, I would./No, I wouldn't.

B. Role Play

**Have students role play a customer and a salesperson in an electronics store. The customer tells the salesperson what he/she wants and asks the price. The salesperson responds. The customer is not sure he/she can afford it. The salesperson tries to convince him/her to buy it.

C. Discussion

**Have students tell which electronic equipment they would like to have and why.

CONSTRUCTION   Page   53

PRIMARY OBJECTIVES

Recognize and describe the construction items on the page.
Recognize and describe the purposes of the tools on the page.

CONVERSATIONAL OBJECTIVES

Talk about personal experience with the objects on the page.
Talk about male and female attitudes toward construction.

RELATED UNITS

Action at the Gym (page 27), **Housing** (page 39), **Tools** (page 50)

VOCABULARY NOTES

Usage

A hard hat is the hat or helmet worn by a construction worker (photo 5). But the term is also used as a word synonymous for *construction worker.*

RELATED IDIOMS AND EXPRESSIONS

to work things out: to solve a problem.
to work up: to develop. Usually used with *a sweat, a thirst,* or *an appetite.*
Rome wasn't built in a day: A serious project takes time to complete.

FURTHER PRACTICE

A. Talk about Construction

*Have students ask each other if they have used construction tools.

     S1: Have you ever used a frontend loader?

     S2: Yes, I have./No, I haven't.

     S2: Have you ever used a jackhammer?

     S1: Yes, I have./No, I haven't.

B. Categorizing

*Have students divide the items on the page into two categories:
1. Tools used for building things: girder, scaffold, cement mixer, etc.
2. Tools used for tearing down things: jackhammer, backhoe, blasting mat, pickax, etc.

C. Discussion

**1. Ask students about their experiences with construction work and other difficult work.

     T: Have you ever done any construction work?
       What did you do?
       Was it difficult work?
       What's the hardest job you've ever had?
       Why was it so hard (physical, long hours, hot)?

**2. Ask students if they think construction work is appropriate for women.

T: Do you think women should do construction work? Why or why not?
  Are there some jobs that women should do and others that women shouldn't do? For example, should women mix cement but not operate a jackhammer?

LAND & WATER

PRIMARY OBJECTIVES

Recognize and describe the land and water scenes on the page.
Talk about locations of nearby landscapes and seascapes.

CONVERSATIONAL OBJECTIVES

Talk about personal experiences with land and water sites.
Talk about famous mountains, forests, rivers, lakes, deserts, and waterfalls.
Express opinions about which type of surroundings students would like to live in.

RELATED UNITS

The World (page 7), **The United States** (page 9), **Canada** (page 10), **The Backyard and Garden** (page 40), **Water Sports** (page 63), **The Zoo & Pets** (page 71), **The Farm** (page 73), **Fish & Sea Animals** (page 74)

CULTURAL COMMENTS

The U.S. has hundreds of parks called national parks, where nature has not been changed. Many Americans go to these parks on vacation. The most famous of these parks are Yellowstone Park, Yosemite Park, Redwood National Park, and the Grand Canyon. People hike, fish, take walks, bird watch, and camp in some of these national parks. They are open to the public for recreation and enjoyment, and are maintained by the U.S. government.

VOCABULARY NOTES

Additional Words

Introduce related verbs to help students describe their experiences with mountains, rivers, streams, and fields: *climb, fish, hike, camp, swim, walk.*

RELATED IDIOMS AND EXPRESSIONS

back-to-nature: used to describe someone or something that uses natural methods rather than technology.
It doesn't hold water: It's not true; it's not valid.
second nature: something done without thinking; instinctually.

MINI-PRACTICE NOTES

Additional Structures

Introduce the singular form.

Is there <u>a mountain</u> near here?
Yes, there is./No, there isn't.
Is there <u>a waterfall</u> near here?
Yes, there is./No, there isn't.

Have students ask each other about the locations of the objects in the pictures.

Where's the <u>mountain</u>?
It's <u>behind the meadow</u>.
Where's the <u>cliff</u>?
It's <u>above the water</u>.

FURTHER PRACTICE (Wall Chart Set 2)

A. Talk about Land and Water

*1. Have students ask each other about land and water in their countries.

S1: Does your country have a lot of <u>mountains</u>?

S2: Yes, it does./No, it doesn't.

**2. Have students ask each other about their experience with the land and water features on the chart.

S1: Have you ever seen a <u>waterfall</u>?

S2: Yes, I have./No, I haven't.

B. Word Association

**Have students look at the photos and tell what word(s) they think of when they see each of the land and water features.

T: What do you think of when you see a <u>mountain</u>?
S1: <u>High/skiing</u>.
S2: <u>Peaks/climbing</u>.

Students can refer to **Weather & Seasons** (page 4), **Opposites** (pages 33 and 34), "**D. Colors**" (pages 35 and 36), **Water Sports** (page 63), and **Winter Sports** (page 64) for additional vocabulary.

C. Discussion

**1. Ask students to describe a famous mountain, forest, river, lake, waterfall, or desert in their country. Have them tell why people visit the famous place.

**2. Ask students where they would like to live and have them tell why.

T: Would you like to live on a mountain?
Would you like to live in a forest?
Would you like to live along a river?
Would you like to live in a desert?

PRIMARY OBJECTIVES

Recognize and describe the car parts and items associated with cars on the page.
Recognize and describe the locations of the parts of the car.
Recognize and describe the types of cars on the page.

CONVERSATIONAL OBJECTIVES

Talk about personal experiences with cars.
Talk about the car students would most like to own.
Talk about buying a car.

RELATED UNITS

The City (page 11), The Train, Bus & Taxi (page 56), Routes & Road Signs (page 57)

CULTURAL COMMENTS

Almost every family in the United States has a car. Some have more than one car. A car is
   a status symbol in the United States. People often judge each other by the car they
   drive.
A stickshift car has a gearshift and a clutch, like the car on the page. An automatic car
   shifts automatically and does not have a gearshift or a clutch. Most American cars are
   automatics. Most foreign cars are stickshifts.
There are several types of gasoline (gas) at a gas station: regular, unleaded, super, and
   diesel. Most cars built before 1973 run on regular. All cars built after 1973 must use
   unleaded gas. Super is better for a car's engine, but costs more. Diesel gas is for vehicles with diesel engines.

VOCABULARY NOTES

Alternate Words

     1—gas station = service station = filling station
    15—fuel gauge = gas gauge
    17—turn signal = directional signal
    38—pick-up truck = pickup

Additional Words

sportscar: a sporty-looking car like a Porsche or a Corvette. It has room for only two
   people.
horn: device on a car that makes a noise when pressed.
gasoline or gas: the fuel that makes a car go.
headlights: lights on the front of the car used for driving at night. Usually referred to in
   the plural.

RELATED IDIOMS AND EXPRESSIONS

car pool: a group of people riding together in one car. People form car pools to save money and gas when going to work or driving children to school.

to floor it (SYNS step on it, step on the gas, put the pedal to the metal): literally, to depress the gas pedal all the way to the floor of the car; drive very fast.

Sunday driver: someone who drives very slowly and cautiously.

MINI-PRACTICE NOTES

Additional Structures

Introduce the following structure:

> Have you ever driven a <u>sedan</u>?
> Yes, I have./No, I haven't.

FURTHER PRACTICE

A. Talk about the Car

*Have students ask each other about the car.

> S1: Where's the <u>clutch</u>?
> S2: It's <u>to the left of the brake.</u>
>
> S2: Where's the <u>alternator</u>?
> S1: It's <u>to the right of the engine.</u>
>
> S3: Where's the <u>taillight</u>?
> S4: It's <u>above the bumper.</u>
>
> S4: Where's the <u>temperature gauge</u>?
> S3: It's <u>below the fuel gauge.</u>

B. Discussion

**1. Ask students if they have ever owned a car. Ask them to describe it.

> T: Have you ever owned a car?
> What kind of car was it: a two-door car, a four-door car, a convertible, or a station wagon?
> What color was it?
> Did it go fast?
> Did you like driving your car?

**2. Ask students to describe the kind of car they would like to own.

> T: What kind of car would you like to own?
> Would it be a convertible?
> Would it be a sportscar like a Porsche or a Ferrari?
> Would it be a luxury car like a Mercedes or a BMW?
> What color would it be?

C. Role Play

**Have students take turns playing a customer and a car salesperson. The salesperson asks what kind of car the customer would like to buy, and how much money he or she wants to spend. The customer asks to test-drive the cars that the salesperson has and asks how much each car costs. The salesperson tells the customer all about the car and tries very hard to sell him or her the car. The customer may buy the car if the price is fair. If he or she thinks the price is not fair, he or she tells the salesman and doesn't buy the car.

THE TRAIN, BUS & TAXI   Page   56

PRIMARY OBJECTIVES

Recognize and describe the items on the page associated with trains, buses, and taxis.
Read a train schedule.
Set up appointments to meet people using the prepositions *at, on, near,* and *under.*

CONVERSATIONAL OBJECTIVES

Talk about personal traveling experiences.
Talk about the train, bus, and taxi using the superlatives *earliest, latest, first,* and *last.*

RELATED UNITS

The Car (page 55), **Routes & Road Signs** (pages 57 and 58), **The Airport** (page 59)

CULTURAL COMMENTS

A person who travels by train to work every day is called a commuter. He or she commutes on a commuter train, which is different from a regular train. A commuter train goes back and forth from a major city to a few suburbs. There are no sleeping compartments on a commuter train. People can also commute to their jobs by bus.

Few Americans travel by train except to commute to the city, although train travel has become more popular in recent years.

People may travel by bus if they cannot afford to fly or take the train, or if they are going someplace where planes or trains do not stop.

VOCABULARY NOTES

Alternate Words

    3—ticket counter = ticket window
   15—taxi = cab = taxicab
    D—schedule = timetable

Additional Words

conductor: the person who drives the train.
ticket clerk: the person who sells passengers tickets for a train (or bus) at the ticket counter.

RELATED IDIOMS AND EXPRESSIONS

on schedule (SYN on time): leaving or arriving at the previously specified time.
every hour on the hour (or on the half-hour): at 6:00, 7:00, 8:00, etc. (on the half-hour: at 5:30, 6:30, 7:30, etc.).
hourly: once every hour.
to catch the train or bus: to board a train or bus.
to miss the train or bus: to fail to catch the train or bus.

MINI-PRACTICE NOTES

Usage

A note on *at, on,* and *in*: We say "at the train station," "at the bus station," and "at the information booth." We say "on the train," "on the track," "on the platform," and "on the bus." We say "in the taxi" and "in the car."

FURTHER PRACTICE (Wall Chart Set 1)

A. Talk about the Schedule

*1. Have students practice reading the train schedule. Ask students to look at the schedule in their book. Then ask questions about arrivals and departures.

    T: The train leaves Pelham at 7:12 A.M. What time does it arrive in New York?

    S: 7:40 A.M.

    T: The train leaves Pelham at 11:33 A.M. What time does it arrive in New York?

    S: 12:03 P.M.

Students can refer to **Time** (page 2) for review of telling time.

*2. Have students ask each other questions about the schedule using superlatives, *the earliest, the latest, the first, the last.*

    S1: When's (what time's) the earliest train to New York on Sundays?

    S2: 7:03 A.M.

    S2: What time's the latest train to New York on Mondays?

    S1: 12:58 A.M.

    S1: What time's the latest train to New York in the morning on Tuesdays?

    S2: 11:33 A.M.

Students can also bring in train, plane, or bus schedules from their own area and practice reading schedules.

B. Role Play

*Talk about prepositions of place, such as *at, near, under,* and *on.* Have students make arrangements to meet each other. They should talk about where and what time they will meet.

S1: Where should we met?

S2: At the information booth/under the clock/near the arrival and departure board.

S1: What time should we meet?

S2: Two o'clock/At two.

C. Discussion

**Ask students questions about their travel experiences.

T: Which do you prefer—traveling by car, bus, train, or plane? Why?

Have students talk about an interesting, exciting, frightening or unusual trip they took by bus, train, or taxi.

ROUTES & ROAD SIGNS   Page   57

PRIMARY OBJECTIVES

Recognize and describe the routes and road signs on the page.
Recognize and describe the action and/or location of the objects on the page.

CONVERSATIONAL OBJECTIVES

Talk about driving experiences.
Talk about driving rules in the U.S. and other countries.

RELATED UNITS

The City (page 11), The Car (page 55), The Train, Bus & Taxi (page 56)

CULTURAL COMMENTS

The Interstate Highway System goes across the United States and is funded by the U.S. government. There are also state and local highways that are paid for by state or local governments because they do not go across state lines. The sign in photo 26 is a route sign for an interstate highway.

When a traffic light has only a red and a green light (as in photo 24), a red light means "stop," a green light means "go," and a red light and a green light at the same time means "slow down." When the traffic light has three lights (as in photo 7 on page 11), a yellow light means "slow down, or proceed with caution." Most traffic lights have red, yellow, and green lights.

The maximum speed limit in the United States is 65 miles per hour (mph). You can drive 65 on large highways in lightly populated areas. But on most highways, the speed limit is 55 mph.

When driving, it is forbidden to cross a double yellow line. Drivers should not cross a solid line, except in an emergency. It is always permitted to cross a broken line, however.

VOCABULARY NOTES

Alternate Words

A—highway = freeway = parkway = expressway
1—overpass = viaduct
6—divider = median
7—left lane = passing lane
8—middle lane = center lane
G—railroad crossing = train crossing
24—traffic light = stoplight
25—railroad track = train track

Usage

*Railroad track (or train track) is a term often used in the plural: Watch out for the railroad tracks.

Additional Words

exit: a road leading off the highway into a city or town.
entrance: a road leading onto a highway from a city or town.
gridlock (see also traffic jam, page 12, photo 19): when cars going in one direction block up an intersection, preventing other cars from crossing the intersection.
speeding ticket: a penalty that the police give a driver who exceeds the speed limit.

RELATED IDIOMS AND EXPRESSIONS

life in the fast lane: living a carefree, irresponsible life.
highway robbery: charging an extremely high price.

MINI-PRACTICE NOTES

Additional Structure

Have students describe the location of the objects on the page, using *to the left of* and *to the right of*.

Where's the car (11)?
It's to the right of the van (10).
Where's the stop sign (27)?
It's to the left of the yield sign (28).

FURTHER PRACTICE (Wall Chart Set 1)

A. Talk about Routes and Road Signs

Point to parts of the pictures and ask students questions about each picture.

T: (Have students look at the first highway picture in scene **A**. Point to the orange car. Then point to the green route sign to Washington Blvd.) Where's the orange car going?
S: To Washington Blvd./To Columbia Pike.
T: How many cars are going to Washington Blvd?
S: Three.

T: (Point to the yellow speed limit sign). What's the speed limit?

S: 35 (miles an hour).

T: (Point to the second highway picture in scene **A**).
Which lane is the van in?

S: The left lane.

T: Which lane is the bus in?

S: The middle lane.

T: Which lane is the truck in?

S: The right lane.

T: (Point to the Tollgate picture **B**).
How much is the toll?

S: $1.25

T: (Point to the Tunnel picture **C**).
Where is the van going?

S: Into the tunnel.

B. Discussion

**Ask students about driving and traffic.

T: Do you drive?
Do you have your own car? What kind is it?
Do you like to drive? Which lane do you like to drive in (or ride in)?
Who usually drives in your family?
What does a broken line mean?
Can you cross a solid line?
What is the shoulder for?
Do you need exact change at a tollbooth?
Are drivers here the same as in your country?

FURTHER PRACTICE (Wall Chart Set 1)

A. Talk about Road Signs

*Point to the signs and ask what they mean.

T: Look at <u>number 30.</u> What does it mean?

B. Giving Directions

**Have students give directions by car to a familiar place in their area. While one student gives the directions, the other students write them down. Discuss whether the directions are understandable, clear, and accurate. Encourage students to use expressions such as *turn left* (at the traffic light), *turn right* (at the stop sign), *go straight* (to the railroad crossing).

C. Discussion

**In small groups, have students answer questions about driving and safety.

T: Do you stop at stop signs?
Do you stop at red lights?
Do you obey speed limit signs?
Have you ever had a speeding ticket? What happened?
Have you ever had an accident? What happened?
Would you stop to help someone in an accident? Why or why not?
Do you prefer driving on city streets, highways, or dirt roads? Why?

THE AIRPORT   Page   59

PRIMARY OBJECTIVES

Recognize and identify the airport terms on the page.

CONVERSATIONAL OBJECTIVES

Talk about personal experiences on planes and in airports.
Practice typical conversations that take place on a plane and in an airport.
Practice typical announcements given by the pilot and crew on an airplane.

RELATED UNIT

The Train, Bus & Taxi (page 56)

CULTURAL COMMENTS

Most Americans have been to an airport and are familiar with the procedures of boarding
a plane.
Members of religious groups and other organizations seeking contributions often solicit
them from travelers in airports.

VOCABULARY NOTES

Alternate Words

3—suitcase = valise
19—customs officer = customs agent
27—overhead (luggage) compartment = overhead bin
34—flight attendant = steward (male) or stewardess (female)

Usage

Luggage is a collective (or mass) noun for *suitcases*:
"How much luggage do you have?"
"I have two suitcases and a briefcase."

Additional Words

duty-free shop: a store at international airports where travelers can buy liquor, cigarettes, perfume, and other gifts without paying import taxes when they bring them to another country.

money exchange: a place to exchange currencies from different countries. Most international airports have money exchange booths.

traveler's aid desk or tourist bureau: a place where travelers can make hotel or restaurant reservations, find out how to rent a car, or get information about the city they have arrived in.

nonstop: a flight that goes directly from one city to another without stopping in between.

stopover or layover: time spent in an airport while waiting to change planes.

RELATED IDIOMS AND EXPRESSIONS

takeoff: the action of leaving the ground and flying into the air. Also used as a verb—to take off: to leave the ground.

MINI-PRACTICE NOTES

Usage

*A note on at, on, and in: We say "at the terminal," "at the gate," "at the check-in counter," and "at the ticket counter." We say "in the cabin," "in the overhead compartment," and "in the cockpit." We say "on the runway," "on the carousel," "on the counter," and "on the tray table."

FURTHER PRACTICE

A. Talk about Flying

*Have students ask each other about flying.

> S1: Have you ever flown before?
>
> S2: Yes, I have.
>
> S1: Do you like to fly?
>
> S2: Yes, I do./No, I don't.
>
> S2: Have you ever flown before?
>
> S1: No, I haven't.
>
> S2: Would you like to fly?
>
> S1: Yes, I would./No, I wouldn't.

B. Discussion

**Ask students to talk about their experiences with planes and airports.

> T: Have you ever been to an airport?
> Have you ever ridden on an airplane? Where did you go?
> Have you ever traveled by plane to another country?
> Have you ever gone into the cockpit?
> Have you ever ridden in a helicopter?
> Do you like airline food?
> Do you usually carry a lot of luggage when you travel?

C. Role Play

**Have students work in groups of five. One student plays the passenger. The other students play the people that a passenger meets on an international plane trip. The ticket agent asks the passenger for his or her ticket, asks if he or she wants to sit in smoking or non-smoking, and gives him or her a boarding pass.
The flight attendant asks the passenger if he or she would like a drink. The flight attendant also asks the passenger what he or she would like for dinner.
The customs officer asks the passenger if he or she has any items to declare, and how long he or she will be staying in the country. The customs officer also asks to see the passenger's passport.
The porter offers to carry the passenger's bags and to get him or her a taxi.

THE WATERFRONT   Page 61

PRIMARY OBJECTIVES

Recognize and describe the waterfront objects on the page.
Recognize and describe the locations of the items on the page.

CONVERSATIONAL OBJECTIVES

Talk about personal experience with travel by boat.

CULTURAL COMMENTS

Travel by ship is very expensive and is therefore becoming quite rare in the United States.
Ferries carry people and cars across rivers or lakes that are too big for a bridge. People who live across a river or lake from a big city often commute by ferry.
A cargo ship, or freighter, may carry a few passengers. It is much less expensive to travel on a freighter than on a cruise ship. But because the main purpose of such a ship is to transport cargo, the ship is not as luxurious. It also may not stick to its original schedule because it can be delayed by its cargo stops. Therefore, passengers who do choose such a ship must have fairly flexible schedules. Passengers on cargo ships are usually college students or retired people.

VOCABULARY NOTES

Usage

A passenger ship is often called a cruise ship. When you ride on a passenger ship, you take a cruise.
Port, starboard, bow, and *stern* are nautical terms for the left side of the boat, the right side of the boat, the front of the boat, and the rear of the boat, respectively. These terms apply to all boats, not only ocean liners.

Additional Words

gangplank, gangway: the ramp you walk up to board a ship.
lifeboat: a small boat kept on a ship in case of emergency.

RELATED IDIOMS AND EXPRESSIONS

to barge in: to enter suddenly and forcefully.
to go off the deep end: to become crazy; act like one who is crazy.

MINI-PRACTICE NOTES

Additional Structure

Introduce the following structure:

> Have you ever seen an oil tanker?
> Yes, I have./No, I haven't.

FURTHER PRACTICE

A. Talk about the Waterfront

*Have students ask questions about the pictures on the page to review their knowledge of prepositions that describe location.

> S1: Where's the tugboat?
>
> S2: It's behind the barge.
>
> S2: Where's the ocean liner?
>
> S1: It's next to the dock.

B. Discussion

**Ask students about their experiences with boats.

> T: Have you ever been on a ship?
> What kind was it?
> Have you ever traveled by ship? Where did you go?
> Do you like to be on boats?
> Do you get seasick?

C. Activity: Name the Ship

**Divide the class into two teams. One student from team A describes a kind of ship seen on the waterfront. One student on team B has to name that kind of ship.

> S1: This ship carries oil.
>
> S2: A tanker.
>
> S3: This ship takes people on long cruises.
>
> S4: An ocean liner.

THE BEACH

PRIMARY OBJECTIVES

Recognize and describe the beach items on the page.
Describe the items students usually take to the beach.

CONVERSATIONAL OBJECTIVES

Talk about things students do on the beach using *always*, *sometimes*, and *never*.
Plan a trip to the beach.

RELATED UNITS

The Waterfront (page 61), Water Sports (page 63)

CULTURAL COMMENTS

Americans often go to the beach when they take a vacation.
Some people never go in the water when they go to the beach. They just lie on the sand
and try to get a tan. Many people in the U.S. think they look better with a tan. However, many people are becoming more aware of the dangers of the sun, so they wear
protective sunscreens and lotions to prevent cancer and other skin diseases caused by too
much sun.

VOCABULARY NOTES

Alternate Words

      6—trash can = garbage can
    13—ocean = sea
    17—bathing suit = swimsuit = bathing trunks (men only)
    19—seashell = shell
    20—rock = stone

Additional Words

suntan lotion/suntan cream/suntan oil/sunscreen: an oil, cream, or lotion people put on their
  bodies to improve their suntan and prevent sunburn.
sunglasses: glasses that protect your eyes from the sun.

RELATED IDIOMS AND EXPRESSIONS

to wash away: to ruin, take away, or destroy.
a drop in the bucket: an unimportant amount.
soaking wet (SYN dripping wet): very wet, dripping water

MINI-PRACTICE NOTES

Additional Structure

Introduce the following structure using *to the left of*, *to the right of*, *in front of*, and *behind*:

Where's the beach hat?
It's to the right of the beach ball.
Where's the trash can?
It's to the left of the umbrella.

FURTHER PRACTICE (Wall Chart Set 2)

A. Talk about the Beach

*Have students ask each other if they like to go to the beach.

S1: Do you like to go to the beach?
S2: Yes, I do./No, I don't.

B. Practice with Adverbs of Frequency

*Ask the students questions about what they do at the beach. Have students answer using an adverb of frequency.

T: Do you ever go to the beach?
S: Yes, I often do.
T: Do you ever swim?
S: No, I rarely do.
T: Do you ever collect seashells?
S: No, I never do.
T: Do you ever play ball on the beach?
  Do you ever build sand castles?
  Do you ever sit in a beach chair?
  Do you ever walk on the boardwalk?
  Do you ever lie on a beach blanket?
  Do you ever lie on the sand?

C. Activity: Find the Details

**Divide the class into two teams. Have students from each team answer the questions below as fast as they can. Decide how much time you will allow for each team to answer (20–30 seconds).

T: How many people are sitting on the green blanket?
  Are they men or women?
  Is the lifeguard a man or a woman?
  What color are the trash cans?
  Where's the green and white umbrella?
  What color are the other umbrellas?
  Are the people on the lounge chairs men or women?

D. Role Play

**Have students work in pairs. One student invites the other to the beach. They talk about what each one would like to bring: a beach ball, a blanket, an umbrella, a picnic lunch, and so on. Students should also decide where to meet.

E. Discussion

**Divide the class into groups. Have each group plan an outing at the beach. One person from each group then reports the plans of the entire group.

Guidelines for discussions are:

What time will the outing be?
Can people bring a friend?
What should people wear?
Will there be music?
Will there be a lifeguard?
Will there be a picnic?
Will there be a barbecue?
Should people bring their own food, or should
everyone contribute money to buy food for the group?
Will there be swimming?
Will there be games? What kind of games?
Will there be lounge chairs?
Should people bring towels or blankets?
What else should people bring?

WATER SPORTS   Page   63

PRIMARY OBJECTIVES

Recognize and describe the sports and equipment on the page.
Recognize and describe the uses of the equipment on the page.

CONVERSATIONAL OBJECTIVES

Talk about personal experiences with various water sports.
Talk about water sports in the U.S. and other countries.
Talk in detail about the pictures on the page.

RELATED UNITS

The Beach (page 62), Winter Sports (page 64), Spectator Sports (page 65), Other Sports (page 67)

CULTURAL COMMENTS

Swimming, fishing, diving, surfing, windsurfing, waterskiing, and sailing are all competitive sports as well as sports that people do for pleasure.

VOCABULARY NOTES

Usage

Both the equipment and the person using the equipment are called a windsurfer.

Windsurfing is also called sailboarding in some parts of the country. In this case, the equipment is called a sailboard and the person is called a sailboarder.

A person who uses a sailboat is often called a sailor. Generally, however, the term *sailor* is reserved for people who have a great expertise at the sport, those who sail professionally, or those who are in the navy.

Additional Words

Introduce verb forms for each sport.

A. swim: I like to swim.
B. dive: I like to dive.
C. snorkel: I like to snorkel.
D. scuba dive: I like to scuba dive.
E. fish: I like to fish.
F. surf: I don't know how to surf.
G. windsurf: Do you know how to windsurf?
H. sail: I don't know how to sail. Do you?
I. waterski: Can you waterski?
J. row: Row the boat as fast as you can.
K. canoe (*go canoeing* is more common): Let's go canoeing.
L. kayak (*go kayaking* is more common): Let's go kayaking.
M. raft (*go rafting* is more common): Let's go rafting.

RELATED IDIOMS AND EXPRESSIONS

in deep water: in great trouble or danger.
up the creek without a paddle: in a hopeless situation.

MINI-PRACTICE NOTES

Using the verbs in the Additional Words section, introduce the structure *Do you like to-infinitive?*

> Do you like to swim?
> Yes, I do./No, I don't.
> Do you like to snorkel?
> Yes, I do./No, I don't.

FURTHER PRACTICE (Wall Chart Set 2)

A. Talk about Water Sports

*Have students ask each other about the water sports on the chart.

> S1: Have you ever tried <u>scuba diving</u>?
> S2: Yes, I have.
> S1: Did you like it?
> S2: Yes, I did./No, I didn't.

S2: Have you ever tried <u>sailing</u>?

S1: No, I haven't.

S2: Would you like to?

S1: Yes, I would./No, I wouldn't.

B. Activity: What Do I Need?

*Divide the class into two teams, or students can work in pairs. One student from team A names a water sport from the chart. A student from team B quickly lists all the equipment needed to perform that sport.

S1: I want to go <u>scuba diving</u>. What do I need?

S2: <u>A wet suit, an air tank, and a mask.</u>

S2: I want to go <u>fishing</u>. What do I need?

S1: <u>A fishing rod and a line.</u>

C. Activity: What Do You See?

Divide the class into two teams. Have students take turns choosing a photo from the chart and describing what they see. Students get a point for each noun and each adjective.

S: I see a man in a red canoe. He's on a lake. He's wearing a white hat and a plaid shirt. He's holding a wooden paddle. (10 points)

Students can refer to **Men's Wear** (page 35), **Women's Wear** (page 36), **Men's & Women's Wear** (page 37), and **Land & Water** (page 54) for additional vocabulary.

D. Discussion

**1. Have students talk about the sport on the chart that they would most like to try, and the sport they would least like to try. They should tell why they are or are not interested in the sport.

**2. Ask students about water sports in their countries.

T: Which water sports do you have in your country?
Which are the most popular?
What kind of people participate in these sports?
Have you done any of these sports? Which ones?

WINTER SPORTS   Page 64

PRIMARY OBJECTIVES

Recognize and describe the winter sports and equipment on the page.
Express preferences among winter sports.

CONVERSATIONAL OBJECTIVES

Talk about personal experiences with winter sports.
Talk in detail about the pictures on the page.

RELATED UNITS

Weather & Seasons (page 4), **Water Sports** (page 63), **Spectator Sports** (page 65), **Other Sports** (page 67)

CULTURAL COMMENTS

Most winter sports are extremely expensive in the United States because they require a great amount of special equipment. They are practiced by a smaller percentage of the population than most other sports. Very few Americans practice bobsledding or snowmobiling.

Sledding is done by almost all children who live in parts of the United States where it snows.

VOCABULARY NOTES

Alternate Words

     1—sled = toboggan
     B—downhill skiing = alpine skiing
     C—Cross country skiing = nordic skiing

Usage

The base form of the verbs for all these sports is the same as the noun that describes the principal piece of equipment: *sled, ski, figure skate, ice skate, bobsled,* and *snowmobile.*

Additional Words

snow: the surface on which you ski and sled.
slope: the trail in downhill skiing.
skating rink: a place to ice skate or figure skate.

RELATED IDIOMS AND EXPRESSIONS

to make a mountain out of a molehill: to exaggerate; make a big problem out of a little one.
to snowball: to develop into something more serious.
on thin ice: in a dangerous situation.

MINI-PRACTICE NOTES

Alternate Structures

Introduce the following structure:

    Do you like <u>downhill skiing</u>?
    Yes, I do./No, I don't. I prefer <u>cross country skiing</u>.

FURTHER PRACTICE (Wall Chart Set 2)

A. Talk about Winter Sports

*Have students ask each other about the winter sports on the chart.

S1: Have you ever tried <u>downhill skiing</u>?

S2: Yes, I have.

S1: Did you like it?

S2: Yes, I did./No, I didn't.

S2: Have you ever tried <u>ice skating</u>?

S1: No, I haven't.

S2: Would you like to?

S1: Yes, I would./No, I wouldn't.

B. Activity: What Do You See?

**Divide the class into two teams. Have students take turns choosing a photo from the chart and describing what they see. Students get a point for each noun and each adjective.

S: I see a man and a woman cross country skiing. They're in a forest. They both have skis and poles. She's wearing a white ski cap, a gray jacket, and gray and blue pants. He's wearing a red ski cap, a gray jacket, and gray and red pants. There's snow on the ground, and the trees have snow on them too. (25 points)

Students can refer to **Men's Wear** (page 35), **Women's Wear** (page 36), **Men's & Women's Wear** (page 37), and **Land & Water** (page 54) for additional vocabulary.

C. Discussion

**1. Have students talk about the sport on the chart that they would most like to try, and the sport they would least like to try. They should tell why they are or are not interested in the sport.

**2. Ask students about winter sports in their countries.

T: Which winter sports are popular in your country?
Which are the most popular?
What kind of people participate in these sports?
Have you done any of these sports? Which ones?

SPECTATOR SPORTS

PRIMARY OBJECTIVES

Recognize and describe the players, sports, and equipment on the page.
Recognize and describe the locations of the players and equipment on the page.

CONVERSATIONAL OBJECTIVES

Talk about personal experiences at a baseball or football game.
Talk about favorite athletes.

RELATED UNITS

Water Sports (page 63), **Winter Sports** (page 64), **Other Sports** (page 67)

CULTURAL COMMENTS

Baseball is called America's pastime and is the most popular sport in the United States. It is also called the summer game because it is played in the summer; baseball players are often called "the boys of summer." Americans have been playing professional baseball for more than 100 years.

Football is the second most popular sport in the U.S. It is played between September and January.

When people go to a baseball game, they almost always eat hot dogs, popcorn, peanuts, and ice cream. At a football game, they generally drink hot chocolate to stay warm.

Soccer is not as popular a spectator sport in the United States as it is in other countries.

VOCABULARY NOTES

Alternate Words

> 16—umpire = ump
> 17—spectator = fan
> 19—batter = hitter
> 43—basket = hoop
> 49—goal = net

Usage

The person who trains and manages a football, basketball, hockey, or soccer team is called the coach. The person who trains and manages a baseball team is called the manager. In baseball, a coach is one of the manager's assistants.

A contest between two baseball, football, basketball, or hockey teams is called a game. In soccer, wrestling, karate, tennis, and boxing, it is called a match, and in horse racing, a race.

Additional Words

score: (n) the number of points each team has in a game; (v) to gain points.
tie (score): situation where each team has the same number of points. (Note: A baseball game can never end in a tie.)
scoreboard: the large board at a stadium that tells the fans what the score is.

RELATED IDIOMS AND EXPRESSIONS

to *shut out*: to prevent the other team from scoring in a game.
Down in front!: a command usually shouted meaning "Sit down!"
box seats: the seats at a stadium nearest the field.

MINI-PRACTICE NOTES

Additional Structures

Introduce the following structure (see the Vocabulary Notes):

> Have you ever been to a tennis match?
> Yes, I have./No, I haven't.

FURTHER PRACTICE (Wall Chart Set 1)

A. Talk about Spectator Sports

*1. Point to the pictures and ask students to name each sport, the players, and the equipment.
   Explain that the word *game* is used with only certain sports: baseball, soccer, (ice) hockey. The word *match* is used with others: wrestling, karate, boxing. *Match* or *game* is used with tennis. Horse racing can also be a horse *race*.

*2. Have students ask each other about the sports on the chart.

> S1: Have you ever seen a <u>basketball game?</u>
>
> S2: Yes, I have./No, I haven't.

**3. Have students ask each other about the sports on the chart and talk about their experiences.

> S1: Have you ever seen a <u>basketball game?</u>
>
> S2: Yes, I have.
>
> S1: When?/Who was playing?/Was it an exciting game?/Where was it?

B. Discussion

**Have students talk about their favorite spectator sport.

> T: What's your favorite sport?
>   Why do you like to watch it?
>   What do the spectators do when they watch these games in your country? Do they yell, cheer, eat hot dogs, sit quietly?
>   Do you ever play any of the games on the chart?

FURTHER PRACTICE (Wall Chart Set 1)

A. Talk about Baseball

*Have students ask and answer questions about the position of the players. Discuss prepositions of place, such as *to the left of, to the right of, in front of, behind, near, on, and at.* Explain that left and right are seen from the vantage point of home plate.

> S1: Where's the first baseman?
> S2: To the left of first base.
> S1: Where's the shortstop?
> S2: To the right of second base.
> S1: No, he isn't. He's to the left of second base.

B. Talk about Football

*Have students ask and answer questions about the position of the players. Discuss prepositions of place, as above. Explain that left and right are seen from the vantage point of the quarterback.

> S1: Where's the center?
> S2: In front of the quarterback.

C. Discussion

**1. Ask students about their experiences at a baseball or football game.

> T: Have you ever seen a baseball/football game?
> Did you enjoy it?
> Which teams were playing?
> What were the spectators like?
> What did the spectators do during the game?
> Are there similar games in your country?

2. Have students talk about their favorite athlete.

> T: What's the name of your favorite athlete?
> What sport does that athlete play?
> Why is that athlete special?

OTHER SPORTS   Page   67

PRIMARY OBJECTIVES

Recognize and describe the sports and equipment on the page.
Express preferences among the sports pictured on the page.

CONVERSATIONAL OBJECTIVES

Talk in detail about the pictures on the page.
Talk about sports students like and dislike.

RELATED UNITS

Water Sports (page 63), Winter Sports (page 64), Spectator Sports (page 65)

CULTURAL COMMENTS

Families often go camping and hiking together. Many families go on camping trips for their vacations. During these trips, they hike, fish, swim, jog, and so on.
Many Americans jog or run to keep in good physical condition.
Few Americans practice archery.

VOCABULARY NOTES

Alternate Words

      3—cyclist = bicyclist
    20—hole = cup
    37—alley = lane

Usage

A bowling alley is both the item pictured in photo 37 and the entire building where you go to bowl.
Handball, racquetball, volleyball, and squash are played on a court. Volleyball can also be played with only a net and a ball on a beach or in a playground.

Additional Words

bullseye: the center of an archery target.
flag: the pole that stands in a golf hole.

RELATED IDIOMS AND EXPRESSIONS

Take a hike! (also, Get lost!): Go away!
It's all downhill from here: The rest is easy.
on target (also, on the mark): exact; precise; perfect.
the ball is in your court: You have to make the decision.

MINI-PRACTICE NOTES

Alternate Structures

Introduce the following structures:

      Do you want to jog?
      No, I'd rather go horseback riding.
      Do you want to play handball?
      No, I'd rather go bowling.

OTHER INFINITIVE FORMS

run/go running   play volleyball
cycle/go cycling/go biking   play squash

shoot arrows/practice archery   play handball
golf/go golfing   play ping pong
rollerskate/go rollerskating   play racquetball
hike/go hiking   camp/go camping

FURTHER PRACTICE (Wall Chart Set 2)

A. Talk about Sports

*Have students ask each other questions using the noun forms for the name of the person who performs the sports on the chart.

    S1: Are you a golfer?

    S2: Yes, I am.

    S1: Do you know any other golfers?

    S1: Yes, I do./No, I don't.

    S2: Are you a hiker?

    S1: No, I'm not.

    S2: Do you know any hikers?

    S1: Yes, I do./No, I don't.

B. Activity: What Do You See?

**Divide the class into two teams. Have students take turns choosing a photo from the chart and describing what they see. Students get a point for each noun and each adjective.

    S: I see a man and a woman jogging on the beach. She's wearing a red shirt. He's wearing a yellow shirt. They're both wearing white shorts. I also see the ocean, waves, and sand. (12 points)

Students can refer to **Men's Wear** (page 35), **Women's Wear** (page 36), **Men's & Women's Wear** (page 37), **Land & Water** (page 54), and **The Beach** (page 62) for additional vocabulary.

C. Discussion

**Have students talk about the sport on the chart that they would most like to try, and the sport they would least like to try. They should tell why they are or are not interested in the sport.

FURTHER PRACTICE (Wall Chart Set 2)

A. Talk about Sports

**1. Have students ask each other about the sports on the chart.

    S1: Do you know how to play ping pong?

    S2: Yes, I do.

    S1: Do you like to play?

    S2: Yes, I do./No, I don't.

    S2: Do you know how to play racquetball?

    S1: No, I don't.

S2: Would you like to learn?

S1: Yes, I would./No, I wouldn't.

B. Discussion

**1. Ask students to look at the chart and name as many sports as they can that use the same kind of equipment.

T: Which sports use a racket?

S: Squash/racquetball.

T: Which sports use a net?

S: Volleyball/ping pong.

T: Which sports use a ball?

S: Volleyball/bowling/ping pong/handball/squash/racquetball.

**2. Have students look at photos I, L, M, N, and O. Ask students to describe who is about to get the ball in each picture. They can describe this player by position (on the left, on the right) or by clothing (in the green shirt).

T: Who's going to get the ball in picture I?

S: Number 1 in the red shirt.

T: Who's going to get the ball in picture O?

S: The player in front/The player in the yellow shirt.

**3. Have students talk about the sport on the chart that they should most like to try, and the sport they would least like to try. They would tell why they are or are not interested in the sport.

**4. Have students talk about the sports on the chart that are popular in their countries.

T: Are any of these sports popular in your country?
Are they played indoors or outdoors?
Do both men and women play?
Are some of the sports only for young people? Which ones?

ENTERTAINMENT   Page   69

PRIMARY OBJECTIVES

Recognize and describe the entertainers and different forms of entertainment on the page.

CONVERSATIONAL OBJECTIVES

Talk about personal experiences with various forms of entertainment.
Express preferences among forms of entertainment.
Write a movie review in groups.

RELATED UNIT

Musical Instruments (page 70)

CULTURAL COMMENTS

The symphony, opera, ballet, and theater are considered sophisticated entertainment. It is
    fairly expensive to go to the opera, ballet, or the theater in the U.S. Movies and rock
    concerts are considered more popular forms of entertainment. Rock concerts are usually
    preferred by young people.
Men usually wear a coat and tie and women usually dress formally when they go to the
    symphony, opera, ballet, or theater. People usually dress informally when they go to a
    movie or rock concert.

VOCABULARY NOTES

Usage

We usually say "I'm going to *the* symphony" or to *the* opera," or "to *the* ballet."
We often say "I'm going to the theater" or "I'm going to the movies, but "I'm going to *a*
    play" or "I'm going to *a* movie."
Cinema is often used in the names of movie theaters.

Additional Words

movie: the feature at a movie theater.
microphone/mike: a device used to amplify the sound of a person's voice.
row: a horizontal line of seats facing the stage.
costume: the clothes actors wear to make them look like the characters they are portraying.

RELATED IDIOMS AND EXPRESSIONS

to play: to show (at a movie theater)
Break a leg!: entertainers say this before a performance to wish each other good luck.
to bring the house down: to win great admiration from the audience.
standing ovation: when people in the audience stand and clap as a sign of appreciation
    and respect for a performance or actor.
standing room only crowd/full house/packed house/sold out: terms referring to a theater that
    has sold all its tickets and is full of people.

MINI-PRACTICE NOTES

Additional Structure

Introduce the following structure:

> Would you like to go to the theater?
> Yes, I would./No, I wouldn't.

FURTHER PRACTICE

A. Talk about Entertainment

*Have students ask each other about various forms of entertainment.

> S1: Have you ever been to a <u>symphony</u>?
>
> S2: Yes, I have.
>
> S1: Did you enjoy it?

S2: Yes, I did./No, I didn't.

S2: Have you ever been to an <u>opera</u>?

S1: No, I haven't.

S2: Would you like to go?

S1: Yes, I would./No, I wouldn't.

B. Discussion

**Ask students to talk about their feelings about different forms of entertainment.

T: If you could be any kind of entertainer, what kind would you be: a dancer, a singer, an actor, a musician? Why?
What's your favorite form of entertainment?
Who's your favorite actor?
Who's your favorite singer?
Who's your favorite dancer?
Who's your favorite conductor?

C. Activity: Movie Review

**Divide the class into groups of two or three. Ask each group to choose a movie that everyone in the group has seen. Students write a review of it. A movie review should include the following: a summary of the plot; the names of the actors in the movie; an evaluation of the acting; an evaluation of the movie overall; the reviewer's recommendation.
When the groups have finished, one member of each group reads the review aloud to the class.

MUSICAL INSTRUMENTS Page 70

PRIMARY OBJECTIVES

Recognize and describe the musical instruments on the page.
Use *larger than* and *smaller than* to describe sizes of musical instruments.

CONVERSATIONAL OBJECTIVE

Talk about personal experiences with musical instruments.

RELATED UNIT

Entertainment (page 69)

CULTURAL COMMENTS

The violin, viola, cello, and bass are the instruments of a string quartet.

The guitar is played with a pick. All the other string instruments on the page are played with a bow.

The words *strings*, *brass*, *woodwinds*, and *percussion* also refer to the major parts or sections of an orchestra.

The guitar, drum, cymbal, harmonica, and sometimes the accordion are instruments used in rock and roll music. The saxophone, bass, and piano are used in all kinds of music. All the other instruments on the page are usually used only in symphonies and classical music. The violin is used in classical music as well as in the typically U.S. music known as country & western music, where it is usually called a fiddle.

VOCABULARY NOTES

Usage

A drum kit, or the drums, is a set of several drums and cymbals.
A keyboard is an electronic instrument with a sound that resembles that of a piano.
Mouth organ is the professional term for *harmonica*.
The saxophone is often referred to as simply the sax.

RELATED IDIOMS AND EXPRESSIONS

to blow your own horn: to boast or brag of your achievements.
to drum up: to create, find

MINI-PRACTICE NOTES

Additional Structure

Have students describe the locations of the instruments using *to the left of*, *to the right of*, *above*, and *below*.

> Where's the trombone?
>
> It's above the French horn and the tuba.

FURTHER PRACTICE

A. Talk about Musical Instruments

Have students ask each other if they play any musical instruments.

> S1: Do you play the flute?
>
> S2: Yes, I do./No, I don't.
>
> S2: Do you play the guitar?
>
> S1: Yes, I do./No, I don't.

B. Discussion

**Ask students if they play a musical instrument.

> T: Do you play a musical instrument? Which one?
> How long have you played it?
> Have you ever performed for other people?
> If you don't play a musical instrument, which instrument would you like to be able to play? Why?

Do you know someone who plays this instrument?
Do you know someone who could teach you how to play this instrument?

C. Role Play

**Have students work in pairs, taking turns playing a streetcorner musician and a police officer. The musician is playing the guitar in public and collecting money from passersby. The police officer says he or she cannot play on the corner because the music is disturbing people who live in the neighborhood. The musician argues with the police officer for a while. Then he or she leaves, but as soon as the police officer goes away, the musician returns.

THE ZOO & PETS   Page 71

PRIMARY OBJECTIVES

Recognize and describe the animals on the page.
Recognize and describe characteristics of the animals on the page.
Categorize animals according to habitat, appearance, and speed.

CONVERSATIONAL OBJECTIVES

Talk about personal experiences with zoo animals and pets.
Express preferences among zoo animals and pets.

RELATED UNITS

The Farm (page 73), Fish & Sea Animals (page 74), Birds (page 75)

CULTURAL COMMENTS

Many people think zoos are cruel to animals because the animals are kept in cages, as though they were in prison. Other people like zoos because zoos provide an opportunity to see wild animals like lions, tigers and bears, and to see animals from other parts of the world like camels, giraffes, zebras, kangaroos, llamas, and polar bears.

There are now some zoos which allow the animals to run free; visitors view the animals from their cars.

Some verbs used to describe the noises made by animals are as follows: Lions, tigers, and leopards roar; bears and polar bears growl; snakes hiss; dogs bark; cats meow; parakeets chirp.

The most popular pets in the U.S. are dogs and cats. Some people, usually children, have hamsters, gerbils, guinea pigs, fish, turtles, or parakeets as pets. Very few people have parrots as pets, and even fewer have snakes and frogs as pets.

People in the U.S. and Canada generally treat their pets as family members and feed them well. It would normally be unthinkable to eat a dog or cat in the U.S., yet many people eat rabbit.

VOCABULARY NOTES

Alternate words

11—rhinoceros = rhino
13—hippopotamus = hippo
16—buffalo = bison
22—deer = doe (female), stag (male)
42—cat = pussycat
50—rabbit = bunny

Additional Words

cub: a young bear.
fawn: a young deer.

RELATED IDIOMS AND EXPRESSIONS

to monkey around/horse around: to waste time by acting silly.
the straw that broke the camel's back (also, the last straw): the point at which a certain behavior or action becomes excessive or intolerable.
to let the cat out of the bag (SYN to spill the beans): to reveal a secret or surprise.

MINI-PRACTICE NOTES

Additional Structures

Introduce the following structures:

Do you have a pet?
Yes, I do.
What kind of pet do you have?
A cat.
Do you have a pet?
No, I don't.
Would you like to have one?
Yes, I would./No, I wouldn't.

FURTHER PRACTICE (Wall Chart Set 1)

A. Talk about Animals

*1. Ask students to look at the chart and name the animals that come from their country.
**2. Have students ask each other about their experiences with animals.

S1: Have you ever seen a deer?

S2: Yes, I have.

S1: Did you see it in a zoo?

S2: Yes, I did./No, I didn't. I saw it in the forest.

S2: Have you ever seen a koala bear?

S1: No, I haven't.

S2: Which animals (on the chart) have you seen?

S1: I saw a camel in the zoo.

B. Categorizing

**Have students work together to put animals into categories:
1. Desert animals/Forest animals/Water animals/Mountain animals
2. Animals with horns (tusks, antlers)/Animals without horns
3. Fastest animals/Slowest animals

C. Discussion

**Have students talk about which animals they like best and which animals they like least. Have them explain why they like or dislike those animals.

FURTHER PRACTICE (Wall Chart Set 1)

A. Talk about Animals

*1. Ask students to look at the chart, write the names of the animals, and put the names in alphabetical order: *alligator, cat, dog*, etc.
**2. Have a student select one of the animals on the chart and describe it to the class. The student can describe the pet by size, color, the sound it makes, where it usually lives, and what it usually eats, but not by name. Other students guess which animal is being described.

Students can refer to "D. Colors" (pages 35 and 36), **Fruit** (page 15), **Vegetables** (page 16), **The World** (page 7 and 8), **The United States** (page 9), **Canada** (page 10), and **Land & Water** (page 54) for vocabulary.

B. Discussion

**Have students describe their pets to each other. If they don't have a pet, they can talk about a pet they have had or would like to have. Encourage students to be as detailed as possible. They could talk about the name of the pet and how it was selected, its special tricks, appearance, peculiar habits, etc.

THE FARM   Page   73

PRIMARY OBJECTIVES

Recognize and describe the farm animals and equipment on the page.
Make comparisons between animals using *older than* and *younger than*.
Describe the items in the photos using prepositions of place.

CONVERSATIONAL OBJECTIVES

Talk about human imitations of animal sounds in English and other languages.
Talk about personal experiences with farm life and farm animals.

RELATED UNITS

The Zoo & Pets (page 71), **Fish & Sea Animals** (page 74), **Birds** (page 75)

CULTURAL COMMENTS

In the 1700s and 1800s, many Americans lived and worked on small farms. Today, only a
small number of people live and work on farms, and the farms are much larger.
Most farms today are commercial farms and specialize in one type of farming. For example, there are wheat farms, corn farms, dairy farms, pig farms, and chicken farms.

VOCABULARY NOTES

Additional Words

livestock: a collective noun for farm animals like pigs and chickens which are raised and
sold for profit.
cattle: a collective word for many cows

Usage

A pig is often called a hog. A female pig is called a sow.

RELATED IDIOMS AND EXPRESSIONS

to be a pig (SYN to be a hog): to take more than you should. Used especially with food.
to pig out: to overeat.
to get one's goat: to bother or annoy someone.
a horse of a different color: an entirely different issue.

MINI-PRACTICE NOTES

Additional Structures

Introduce the following structure:

Have you ever seen a horse?
Yes, I have./No, I haven't.

FURTHER PRACTICE (Wall Chart Set 2)

A. Talk about the Farm

*Have students ask and answer questions about the location of things on the chart. Review
prepositions of place, such as in, to the left of, to the right of, in front of, behind, and near.

S1: Where's the silo?

S2: To the right of the barn.

S2: Where are the pigs?

S1: In the pigpen.

B. Discussion

*1. Talk about how we describe animal sounds in different languages. In English, we say
that a rooster says "cockadoodle doo." In Spanish, for example, a rooster says "keek ee
ree kee." Give the students the animal sounds in English for animals on the chart.
Then ask students about the sounds in their languages for these animals.

T: In English, a horse says "neigh." What does a horse say in your language?
(A pig says "oink," a cow says "moo," a sheep says "baa," a hen says "cluck," a chick says "peep.")

**2. Have students talk about farm life. Some of the students may have grown up on a farm and can speak from personal experience. Others may never have been on a farm and will have to give opinions based only on conjecture.

T: Would you like to be a farmer?
Is the job of a farmer easy?
What's good about farm life?
What's bad about farm life?
What does a farmer do every day?

FISH & SEA ANIMALS   Page 74

PRIMARY OBJECTIVES

Recognize and describe the animals on the page.
Compare the sizes of the animals on the page using the superlative *biggest*.

CONVERSATIONAL OBJECTIVES

Talk about personal experiences with fish and sea animals.
Discuss and prepare recipes for cooking fish.

RELATED UNITS

The Zoo & Pets (page 71), **The Farm** (page 73), **Birds** (page 75)

CULTURAL COMMENTS

Americans cook and eat bass and trout but not sunfish or angelfish. Among the sea animals, the most popular ones to cook and eat are the shellfish (items 21–26). Dolphin is rarely eaten. Seal and walrus are almost never eaten. Starfish are inedible.
Most Americans eat their fish fried, broiled, or baked. Only recently have Americans tried raw fish, in the form of Japanese sushi and sashimi.

VOCABULARY NOTES

Additional Words

Shellfish/seafood: a collective term for items 21–24 and 26.

RELATED IDIOMS AND EXPRESSIONS

to clam up: to suddenly become quiet.

Something's fishy: Something isn't right.
a whale of a . . . : tremendous; great; big.

MINI-PRACTICE NOTES

Alternate Structures

Explain that *large* is a synonym for *big*. Then repeat the mini-practice structure using *largest* instead of *biggest*.

Explain that *small* is the opposite of *big* and *large*. Then repeat the structure in the mini-practice using *smallest* instead of *biggest*.

FURTHER PRACTICE (Wall Chart Set 2)

A. Talk about Fish and Sea Animals

*1. Have students ask each other about their experiences with fish and sea animals.

    S1: Have you ever seen a <u>shark</u>?

    S2: Yes, I have./No, I haven't.

*2. Have students ask each other if they have ever eaten various types of fish on the chart.

    S1: Have you ever eaten <u>shark</u>?

    S2: Yes, I have.

    S1: Did you like it?

    S2: Yes, I did./No, I didn't.

    S2: Have you ever eaten <u>clams</u>?

    S1: No, I haven't.

    S2: Would you like to?

    S1: Yes, I would./No, I wouldn't.

B. Activity: Making a Fish Dish

**Divide the class into small groups. Have each group write a recipe for a fish dish—either cooked or uncooked. Ask one person in each group to read the recipe to the class. Have the students choose the fish dish they would most like to eat.

You might want to introduce such verbs as *clean, scale, mix, stir, slice, cut, bake, broil, boil, fry,* and *deep-dry*.

Students can refer to **The Supermarket** (pages 13 and 14), **Vegetables** (page 16), and **Kitchenware** (page 46) for additional vocabulary.

C. Discussion

**Have students choose a fish or sea animal from the chart and describe it.

    S1: (number 9) An angelfish is small and pretty. It's black with yellow stripes.

    S2: (number 21) A lobster has long claws. It's red and tastes delicious.

BIRDS

PRIMARY OBJECTIVES

Recognize and describe the birds on the page.
Recognize and describe characteristics of the birds on the page.
Categorize birds into groups by ability to fly and swim.

CONVERSATIONAL OBJECTIVES

Express opinions about birds.
Talk about personal experiences with birds.

RELATED UNITS

The Zoo & Pets (page 71), **The Farm** (page 73)

CULTURAL COMMENTS

A bald eagle is an eagle with a white head. It is a symbol of America and of freedom. There are very few bald eagles left in the world, and they are protected by the U.S. government as an endangered species.

VOCABULARY NOTES

Usage

A hawk trained to hunt is called a falcon.
An all-white pigeon is called a dove. A dove is a symbol of peace.
Ducklings are young ducks.

RELATED IDIOMS AND EXPRESSIONS

early bird: someone who gets up or arrives early.
for the birds: silly, pointless, or ridiculous.
to eat like a bird: to eat very little.
to kill two birds with one stone: to get two results with one action.
A bird in the hand is worth two in the bush: It is better to definitely have something than to have only the possibility of something else, even if the something else is better than what you already have.
as the crow flies: directly; in a straight line.

MINI-PRACTICE NOTES

Additional Structure

Introduce the following structure:

> Have you ever seen a peacock?
> Yes, I have./No, I haven't.

FURTHER PRACTICE

A. Talk about Birds

*Have students ask each other questions about characteristics of the birds pictured in the unit.

> S1: Does a pelican have flippers?
>
> S2: Yes, it does.
>
> S2: Does an eagle have a bill?
>
> S1: No, it doesn't. (It has a beak.)

B. Discussion

**Have students tell their feelings about birds.

> T: Do you like birds?
> What's your favorite bird?
> What's the prettiest bird?
> Do you like pigeons?
> Which birds have you seen before?
> Which birds have you never seen before?
> Are you a birdwatcher? Where do you go to watch birds?

C. Categorizing

*Have students work together to put birds into categories:
  1. Birds that swim
  2. Birds that fly
  3. Birds that cannot fly or swim

D. Activity: Name the Bird

**Divide the class into two teams. One student on team A describes a bird. One student on team B has to name that bird.

> S1: This bird is white and has a long neck. It also has very long legs for walking in water.
>
> S2: A flamingo.
>
> S2: This bird is black and white and has short legs. It has flippers and lives in cold places.
>
> S1: A penguin.

INSECTS & RODENTS

PRIMARY OBJECTIVES

Recognize and describe the insects and rodents on the page.
Talk about experiences with insects and rodents.

CONVERSATIONAL OBJECTIVES

Talk about fears of insects and rodents.
Discuss hiring an exterminator to kill insects and rodents.

RELATED UNIT

The Zoo & Pets (page 71)

CULTURAL COMMENTS

Most Americans are afraid of rats, bees, and cockroaches. They do not like most insects or
rodents, especially flies, spiders, and mosquitos. They try to kill ants and flying insects
with poisonous spray, and roaches and rats with traps.
Moths make holes in many fabrics. We try to kill moths with mothballs.

VOCABULARY NOTES

Usage

A household "pest" may be an insect or a rodent. The term usually refers collectively to
rats, mice, ants, flies, cockroaches, and spiders.
Bug is a common way of saying "insect," suggesting something you find in your house. An
insect is something you find outdoors or in a nature laboratory.
The plural of mouse is mice.

Additional Words

furry (also, fuzzy): refers to an animal that has thick hair. It also suggests an animal that
you would like to touch. Thus, a guinea pig is usually considered furry, but a rat is not.
to buzz: to make a noise like that of a fly.
web, spiderweb, or cobweb: the net that a spider builds to trap insects.
sting: a bite or wound by insects such as bees or ants.

RELATED IDIOMS AND EXPRESSIONS

to make a beeline: to go directly, without stopping on the way.
to squirrel away: to hide something for later use.

MINI-PRACTICE NOTES

Alternate Structure

*Introduce the plural form.

> Are those <u>bees</u> or flies?
> They're <u>bees</u>.
> Are those <u>rats</u> or <u>mice</u>?
> They're <u>mice</u>.

FURTHER PRACTICE

A. Talk about Insects and Rodents

*Have students ask each other about insects and rodents.

> S1: Have you ever seen a <u>ladybug</u>?
> S2: Yes, I have./No, I haven't.
> S2: Have you ever seen a <u>chipmunk</u>?
> S1: Yes, I have./No, I haven't.

B. Discussion

**Have students discuss their feelings about insects and rodents.

> T: Are you afraid of insects? Which ones? Why?
> Are you afraid of rodents? Which ones? Why?
> What else are you afraid of?

C. Role Play

**Have students work in pairs, taking turns playing an exterminator and a customer who wants to get rid of cockroaches and mice from his or her apartment. The exterminator asks the customer what the problem is. The exterminator says he or she can get rid of the mice and the cockroaches. The customer asks how much it will cost.

SPACE   Page 77

PRIMARY OBJECTIVES

Recognize and describe the planets, equipment, and spacecraft on the page.
Recognize and describe the sizes of the various objects using *bigger* and *smaller*.

CONVERSATIONAL OBJECTIVES

Talk about personal experiences with space and spacecraft.
Express opinions about space exploration.

RELATED UNIT

The Military (page 78)

CULTURAL COMMENTS

People in the United States are still amazed by the progress of space travel in relation to other advances of technology. We often remark that we can put a man on the moon, but we still can't cure the common cold.

Astronauts are national heroes in the United States. People often watch launches and landings of space vehicles on television and cheer the astronauts who go into space.

VOCABULARY NOTES

Usage

Space is sometimes called outer space: The astronauts are going into outer space to explore.

When you can see the whole moon at night (as in photo 7), it is called a full moon. When you cannot see the moon at all, it is called a new moon.

Saturn is the name of the planet in photo 5.

Additional Words

telescope (see page 79): an instrument that uses lenses and/or mirrors to make distant objects appear closer. People use telescopes to look at the stars at night.

shooting star or meteor: a star that moves across the sky.

solar system: a group of planets that revolve around one star. Our solar system includes the moon, the sun, and the nine planets that revolve around it: Mercury, Venus, Earth, Mars, Jupiter, Saturn, Uranus, Neptune, and Pluto.

astronomy: the science of stars and their motions. Astronomy should not be confused with astrology, which is the study of the signs of the zodiac and how the stars and planets influence human behavior. Most people do not consider astrology to be a serious field of study.

RELATED IDIOMS AND EXPRESSIONS

space cadet (slang): a person who is forgetful, does strange things, or who seems to ignore the world around him or her. Such a person may also be described as "spacy" or "spaced out."

once in a blue moon: rarely.

MINI-PRACTICE NOTES

Additional Structures

Have students describe the locations of the items in the lower left (items 7–12) and lower right (items 14–16) photos, using any prepositions of location that they know.

Where's the astronaut?
He's to the left of the flag.
Where's the lunar vehicle?
It's in front of and to the right of the lunar module.

FURTHER PRACTICE

A. Talk about Space

*Have students ask each other questions about space.

> S1: Is a <u>galaxy</u> bigger than a star?
>
> S2: Yes, it is.
>
> S2: Is <u>the Moon</u> bigger than the Earth?
>
> S1: No, it's smaller.

B. Discussion

**Ask students to talk about space and space exploration.

> T: Are you interested in the stars and space? What interests you most?
> Would you like to go to another planet?
> Do you think there's life on other planets?
> Is it important to study space and the stars?
> Is it important to send space shuttles and satellites to other planets to do research?
> Why?

C. Activity: Alien Observations

**Divide the class into small groups. Each group should pretend they are creatures from another planet. They should write down the things that creatures from another planet would notice on their first trip to the planet Earth. When all the groups are finished, one student from each group reads the "alien observations" aloud to the class.

THE MILITARY   Page   78

PRIMARY OBJECTIVES

Recognize and describe the military personnel and equipment on the page.
Recognize and describe the uses for the military equipment on the page.

CONVERSATIONAL OBJECTIVES

Talk about personal experience with the military service.
Debate whether women should serve in the armed forces.

RELATED UNIT

Space (page 77)

CULTURAL COMMENTS

Military service is not currently required in the U.S. But when they turn 18, all male citizens of the U.S. must register for the armed services. Women may join the armed services, but they are not required to do so.

The army is the largest branch of the armed forces. The marines is the smallest.
People in the armed services use a 24-hour (rather than 12-hour) clock. Thus, 7:30 P.M. is
19:30 hours in the armed services. Also, 6:00 A.M. is 06:00 in the military and is said
"oh six hundred hours."

VOCABULARY NOTES

Usage

The army fights on the ground. The navy fights on the sea. The air force fights in the air.
The marines fight on land, sea, and in the air.
Camouflage is a pattern used to disguise soldiers' uniforms so that they blend in with the
grass, trees, and other natural surroundings. The soldier is wearing a camouflage
helmet in photo 3.
A cannon may be used on a tank or without a tank. Stand-alone cannons are not used
very often anymore, however. Instead, soldiers use bazookas, tubes used for shooting
rockets at the enemy.

Additional Words

war: armed fighting between two or more countries.
peace: calm; the absence of war.
armed forces: collective word for the army, navy, air force, and marines.
civilian: a person who is not in the armed forces.

RELATED IDIOMS AND EXPRESSIONS

bomb: a failure.

MINI-PRACTICE NOTES

Additional Structures

Have students practice using military time. Have one student write a time on the blackboard. Have another student tell what time it is in 12-hour time. Then have a third
student tell what time it is in military, or 24-hour, time.

> S1: (writes) 8:00 A.M.
>
> S2: It's eight o'clock in the morning.
>
> S3: It's oh eight hundred hours.
>
> S2: (writes) 9:45 P.M.
>
> S3: It's nine forty-five at night.
>
> S1: It's twenty-one forty-five hours.

FURTHER PRACTICE

A. Talk about the Military

**Have students ask each other questions about where different military vehicles and
machines are used.

S1: Where is a <u>jeep</u> used?

S2: <u>On the road</u>.

S2: Where is a <u>destroyer</u> used?

S1: <u>In the water</u>.

B. Discussion

**Ask students if they ever served in the military.

> T: Did you ever serve in the army, navy, air force, or marines? For how long?
> Did you fight in any wars?
> Did you get hurt?
> Did you enjoy serving in the military?
> Is military service required in your country? How long must you serve?

C. Activity: Debate

**Divide the class into two teams. One team argues that women should not be allowed to serve in the military. The other team argues that women should be allowed to serve in the military. Only one person from each team speaks at a time. Encourage all students to take part in the debate and to state their reasons for arguing the side they chose.

HOBBIES & GAMES   Page   79

PRIMARY OBJECTIVES

Recognize and describe the hobbies, crafts, and games on the page.
Recognize and use the verb forms for each hobby, crafts or game on the page as introduced in the Additional Words section.

CONVERSATIONAL OBJECTIVES

Talk about personal experiences with hobbies, crafts, and games.
Express preferences among hobbies, crafts, and games.

RELATED UNIT

Occupations (page 21)

CULTURAL COMMENTS

Hobbies and crafts are usually done by individuals. Some people go bird watching or look at the stars through a telescope with someone else, but most people like being alone with their hobby or craft.
Games are usually not played alone. Backgammon, chess, checkers, and Scrabble must be played with two players. To play Monopoly, you need at least two players. There are

more than 100 games you can play with cards. Solitaire is a card game you can play by yourself. Other card games are for two or more people.

Poker, bridge, and gin rummy are among the most popular card games. People often spend an entire evening eating, drinking, and playing cards. Sometimes people play poker or bridge every week at a regularly scheduled time.

VOCABULARY NOTES

Alternate Words

1—coin collecting = numismatics
6—stamp collecting = philately
B—crafts = handicrafts = arts and crafts

Usage

A board and all the pieces of a game are called a set: chess set or Scrabble set. A set of 52 cards is called a deck of cards.

Albums are also used for storing photos. They are called photo albums or scrapbooks.

Binoculars are like two small telescopes attached to each other and are used to see things that are far away. The people in photo 14 are using binoculars to look at birds. People also use binoculars at sports events when their seats are far from the field or court. People use small binoculars called opera glasses when they go to the theater. Binoculars are often referred to as a pair or a set of binoculars.

Additional Words

The following chart lists the verb forms for hobbies and crafts and the noun forms for the performer of the hobby or craft.

coin collecting	collect coins	coin collector
stamp collecting	collect stamps	stamp collector
photography	photograph (take photos)	photographer
astronomy	watch stars	astronomer
bird watching	watch birds	bird watcher
sculpting	sculpt	sculptor
knitting	knit	knitter
weaving	weave	weaver
pottery	pot	potter
painting	paint	painter
woodworking	do woodwork	woodworker
(game name)	play (game name)	(game name) player

MINI-PRACTICE NOTES

Alternate Structures

Continue the mini-practice, substituting *like to play* for *play* in the question, and *I prefer playing* or *I prefer* for *but I play* in the response.

Do you like to play chess?
Yes, I do./No, I don't: I prefer playing backgammon.
Do you like to play checkers?
Yes, I do./No, I don't. I prefer Scrabble.

FURTHER PRACTICE

A. Talk about Hobbies and Crafts

Have students ask each other questions about hobbies and crafts.

> S1: Do you like coin collecting?
> S2: Yes, I do./No, I don't.

B. Categorizing

**Have students work together to put hobbies into categories:

1. Hobbies done only indoors
2. Hobbies done only outdoors
3. Hobbies done both indoors and outdoors

C. Discussion

**Ask students what they like to do in their spare time.

> T: Do you have a hobby? What is it?
> How much time do you spend on your hobby every week?
> Do you spend a lot of money on your hobby?
> Do you like to play games? What games do you like to play?
> What's a very popular card game in your country?

SEWING & SUNDRIES   Page   80

PRIMARY OBJECTIVES

Recognize and describe the sewing and sundry items on the page.
Ask to borrow items.

CONVERSATIONAL OBJECTIVES

Talk about personal experiences with sewing.
Discuss making a suit.

RELATED UNIT

Occupations (page 21)

VOCABULARY NOTES

Usage

Wrapping paper is sometimes referred to as gift-wrap. Gift-wrap is also a verb: Can you gift-wrap that for me? It's a present.
Twine is a little bit thinner than string. Rope is thicker than string.

Additional Words

eraser: the pink rubber part on the top of a pencil.

RELATED IDIOMS AND EXPRESSIONS

to sew up: to capture, win, or gain.

MINI-PRACTICE NOTES

Additional Structure

Introduce the following structure:

> Do you have a <u>sewing machine</u>?
> Yes, I do./No, I don't.

FURTHER PRACTICE

A. Talk about Sewing and Sundries

*Have students ask each other if they know how to use the items in the unit.

> S1: Do you know how to use a <u>sewing machine</u>?
> S2: Yes, I do./No, I don't

B. Discussion

**Ask students about sewing.

> T: Have you ever sewn anything?
> Have you ever used a sewing machine?
> Do you like to knit?
> Do you make your own clothes, or do you buy them?
> Do you think men should sew, or is sewing something only women should do?

C. Role Play

**Have students work in pairs, taking turns playing a customer and a tailor. The customer asks the tailor to make a suit of clothes. The tailor asks the customer what color and pattern he or she wants. The tailor measures the customer for the suit and tells him or her how much it costs. The customer pays for the suit.

APPENDIX

MAJOR LEAGUE BASEBALL

National League
Atlanta Braves
Chicago Cubs
Cincinnati Reds
Houston Astros
Los Angeles Dodgers
Montreal Expos
New York Mets
Philadelphia Phillies
Pittsburgh Pirates
St. Louis Cardinals
San Diego Padres
San Francisco Giants

American League
Baltimore Orioles
Boston Red Sox
California Angels
Chicago White Sox
Cleveland Indians
Detroit Tigers
Kansas City Royals
Milwaukee Brewers
Minnesota Twins
New York Yankees
Oakland Athletics
Seattle Mariners
Texas Rangers
Toronto Blue Jays

NATIONAL FOOTBALL LEAGUE (NFL)

American Football Conference
Buffalo Bills
Cincinnati Bengals
Cleveland Browns
Denver Broncos
Houston Oilers
Indianapolis Colts
Kansas City Chiefs
Los Angeles Raiders
Miami Dolphins
New England Patriots
New York Jets
Pittsburgh Steelers
San Diego Chargers
Seattle Seahawks

National Football Conference
Atlanta Falcons
Chicago Bears
Dallas Cowboys
Detroit Lions
Green Bay Packers
Los Angeles Rams
Minnesota Vikings
New Orleans Saints
New York Giants
Philadelphia Eagles
Phoenix Cardinals
San Francisco 49ers
Tampa Bay Buccaneers
Washington Redskins

NATIONAL BASKETBALL ASSOCIATION
(NBA)

Eastern Conference
Atlanta Hawks
Boston Celtics
Charlotte Hornets
Chicago Bulls
Cleveland Cavaliers
Detroit Pistons
Indiana Pacers
Milwaukee Bucks
New Jersey Nets
New York Knicks
Philadelphia 76ers
Washington Bullets

Western Conference
Dallas Mavericks
Denver Nuggets
Golden State Warriors
Houston Rockets
Los Angeles Clippers
Los Angeles Lakers
Miami Heat
Phoenix Suns
Portland Trailblazers
Sacramento Kings
San Antonio Spurs
Seattle SuperSonics
Utah Jazz

To Be Added in 1989-90 season: Minnesota Timberwolves; Orlando Magic.

NATIONAL HOCKEY LEAGUE (NHL)

Boston Bruins
Calgary Flames
Detroit Red Wings
Hartford Whalers
Minnesota North Stars
New Jersey Devils
New York Rangers
Pittsburgh Penguins
St. Louis Blues
Vancouver Canucks
Winnipeg Jets

Buffalo Sabres
Chicago Blackhawks
Edmonton Oilers
Los Angeles Kings
Montreal Canadiens
New York Islanders
Philadelphia Flyers
Quebec Nordiques
Toronto Maple Leafs
Washington Capitals

PRESIDENTS OF THE UNITED STATES

President	Term
1. George Washington	1789–1797
2. John Adams	1797–1801
3. Thomas Jefferson	1801–1809
4. James Madison	1809–1817
5. James Monroe	1817–1825
6. John Quincy Adams	1825–1829
7. Andrew Jackson	1829–1837
8. Martin Van Buren	1837–1841
9. William Henry Harrison	1841–1841
10. John Tyler	1841–1845
11. James Polk	1845–1849
12. Zachary Taylor	1849–1850
13. Millard P. Fillmore	1850–1853
14. Franklin Pierce	1853–1857
15. James Buchanan	1857–1861
16. Abraham Lincoln	1861–1865
17. Andrew Johnson	1865–1869
18. Ulysses S. Grant	1869–1877
19. Rutherford B. Hayes	1877–1881
20. James Garfield	1881–1881
21. Chester A. Arthur	1881–1885
22. Grover Cleveland	1885–1889
23. Benjamin Harrison	1889–1893
24. Grover Cleveland	1893–1897
25. William McKinley	1897–1901
26. Theodore Roosevelt	1901–1909
27. William Howard Taft	1909–1913
28. Woodrow Wilson	1913–1921
29. Warren G. Harding	1921–1923
30. Calvin Coolidge	1923–1929
31. Herbert Hoover	1929–1933
32. Franklin D. Roosevelt	1933–1945
33. Harry S. Truman	1945–1953
34. Dwight D. Eisenhower	1953–1961
35. John F. Kennedy	1961–1963
36. Lyndon B. Johnson	1963–1969
37. Richard M. Nixon	1969–1974
38. Gerald R. Ford	1974–1977
39. Jimmy Carter	1977–1981
40. Ronald Reagan	1981–1989
41. George Bush	1989–

ABBREVIATIONS

Houses and Apartments (for use with Housing chapter)

A/C	Air Conditioning
BLDG	Building
BR or BDRM-	Bedroom
Ceil	Ceiling
CLST	Closet
DRMN	Doorman
D/R	Dining Room
D/W	Dishwasher
EIK	Eat-in Kitchen
ELEV	Elevator
FLR	Floor
FURN	Furnished
GAR	Garage
INC	included
KIT	Kitchen
LG or LGE	Large
L/R	Living Room
LUX	Luxury
PVT	Private
RM	Room
SQ/FT.	Square Feet
UNFURN	Unfurnished
UTILS	Utilities (gas, electric bills)
WBF	Woodburning Fireplace
W/D	Washer and Dryer
W/W	Wall-to-Wall Carpeting

Cars (for use with The Car chapter)

A/C	Air conditioning
AM/FM SC	AM/FM Stereo Cassette
COND	Condition
DR	Door
EVES	Evenings (Call Eves. Only)
K	Thousand (12K miles)
M	Thousand (see K)
P/B	Power Brakes
P/D	Power Doors
P/S	Power Steering
P/W	Power Windows
SPD	Speed (5-spd)

Help Wanted (for use with Occupations chapter)

ADM.	administrative
ACCT. or ACCT'G	accounting
ASST	assistant
EXEC	executive
EXP	experience
F/T	full-time
INDIV	individual
MIN	minimum
OPPTY	opportunity
P/T	part-time
REQD	required
REQS	requirements
SAL	salary
SEC'Y	secretary
TYP	typing
WK	week
WKDYS	weekdays
WKNDS	weekends
W/P	word processing
WPM	words per minute
YRS	years

WEIGHTS AND MEASURES

Length

U.S.

	Metric
1 inch	2.54 centimeters
1 foot	0.3408 meters
1 yard (3 feet)	0.9144 meters
1 mile	1.609 kilometers
0.001 inches	1 millimeter
0.3937 inches	1 centimeter
39.37 inches (1.094 yards)	1 meter
0.621 miles	1 kilometer

Volume

1 ounce	29.574 milliliters
1 cup (eight ounces)	0.237 liters
1 pint (two cups)	0.473 liters
1 quart (two pints)	0.946 liters
1 gallon (four quarts)	3.785 liters
0.0338 ounces	1 milliliter
1.057 quarts	1 liter
2.642 gallons	1 dekaliter

Weights

1 ounce	28.571 grams
1 pound	453.592 grams
0.035 ounces	1 gram
2.205 pound	1 kilogram